BOONE COUNTY LIBRARY

2040 910 822 819 1

SHAKESPEARE FOR ONE

WITHDRAWN

D1472574

BOONE COUNTY PUBLIC LIBRARY
BURLINGTON, KY 41005
www.bcpl.org

SEP 2 3 2003

Boone County Public Library
7425 U.S. Hwy. 42
Florence, KY 41042

SHAKESPEARE FOR ⊙NE

Women

THE COMPLETE
MONOLOGUES AND
AUDITION PIECES

edited by

DOUGLAS NEWELL

HEINEMANN
PORTSMOUTH, NH

Heinemann
A division of Reed Elsevier Inc.
361 Hanover Street
Portsmouth, NH 03801–3912
www.heinemanndrama.com

Offices and agents throughout the world

© 2002 by Douglas Newell

All rights reserved. No part of this book may be reproduced in any form
or by any electronic or mechanical means, including information storage
and retrieval systems, without permission in writing from the publisher,
except by a reviewer, who may quote brief passages in a review.

Library of Congress Cataloging-in-Publication Data
Shakespeare, William, 1564–1616.
  [Plays. Selections]
    Shakespeare for one : women : the complete monologues and
audition pieces / [edited by Douglas Newell].
      p. cm.
    ISBN 0-325-00487-0 (alk. paper)
      1. Acting—Auditions.   2. Women—Drama.   3. Monologues.
I. Newell, Douglas.   II. Title.

PR2771 .N49 2002
822.3'3—dc21   2002009726

Editor: Lisa A. Barnett
Production: Vicki Kasabian
Cover design: Jenny Jensen Greenleaf
Typesetter: TechBooks
Manufacturing: Steve Bernier

Printed in the United States of America on acid-free paper
06 05 04 03 02 DA 1 2 3 4 5

For Carol . . . who rescued her little brother from the neighbor's garage, and from even worse.

CONTENTS

ACKNOWLEDGMENTS

What would eventually become *Shakespeare for One* was born in a stuffy L.A. basin bungalow, yanked kicking and screaming from the keyboard of a solitary, out-of-work actor searching desperately for a purpose in life. Which is not to say that it wasn't a hoot or that there wasn't a little help along the way.

To Gene Openshaw, an old friend who does so many things so extraordinarily well, I owe heartfelt thanks for providing suggestions, advice, and enthusiasm back when WillyBook routinely tottered near the abyss.

For the loan of his computer to a penniless thespian, I thank John Brady; for nobly taking the heat when I was so tardy in returning that computer, I thank John's son and my chum through thick and thin, Peter Brady.

And finally, for her unwavering support and her inexplicable faith that I would indeed see this quixotic journey through to the very end, I offer both love and gratitude to my true companion, Patty Conroy.

INTRODUCTION

Overview

Each chapter covers one of Shakespeare's plays and starts off with a thumbnail sketch of the story's key developments. Plot details not directly related to the featured monologues are omitted.

Following the synopsis is an abridged cast of characters, listing only those persons who somehow play a role in one or more speeches.

Preceding each monologue is its act, scene, and line number in the play; a description of its physical setting; and a brief account of the action or circumstances that have led to the moment at hand.

Line numbers appearing along the side of each monologue refer to the explanatory notes following that speech.

At the back of the book you will find a guide to the pronunciation of character and location names, as well as other information that might be useful in choosing particular monologues.

The Chosen Few

It only makes sense that one of the first issues to be tackled in putting together a comprehensive collection of monologues is exactly what constitutes a monologue. With *Shakespeare for One*, it wasn't long before a few basic qualifications had emerged:

- First off, the speech had to have some semblance of proper structure; which is to say, it needed a more-or-less functional beginning, middle, and end.
- In addition, the selection being considered could require neither wholesale editing nor the presence of another actor in order for it to work logically or dramatically.
- What's more, it was decided that all monologues should have an estimated

running time of at least one minute; any shorter and they would rarely be of use in the classroom or as an audition piece.

With such minimal guidelines in place, an initial pass through Shakespeare's canon resulted in a cumbersome collection of nearly 200 eligible monologues. After several rounds of culling, a far more manageable assortment of speeches finally emerged from the pack: 88 solid solos for the female actor, every one suitable for audition or classroom use.

Most, but not all, of the also-rans had one or more flaws that rendered them unacceptable for the purposes of this project. For example, a few contenders had the requisite length and structure but, alas, were woefully lackluster affairs whose chief attribute was to wax expository.

Then too, some otherwise promising speeches had to be eliminated because nothing even resembling a serviceable entry and/or exit line could be found. Many more candidates were dismissed because, once removed from their proper context, they retained little to offer in the way of theatrical thrills—no action, no intrigue, nothing.

On the other hand, there were those monologues that, while arguably deficient in one way or another, still seemed all too likeable to simply dismiss out of hand. Wherever such flawed gems popped up, they were duly noted in a list of "Alternates" appearing at chapter's end. Anyone seeking options beyond those presented in *Shakespeare for One* is encouraged to turn to the plays themselves and look into a few of these outtakes.

On Editing Shakespeare

From the very inception of this project there existed an ideal to steadfastly resist altering Shakespeare's text in any appreciable way. It was a fine ideal indeed—and more than a little impractical.

Before long it became clear that unless minor modifications were permitted here and there, a wealth of potentially outstanding material would have to be discarded. Such waste seemed self-defeating, to say the least. After all, *Shakespeare for One* is intended for the actor, not the scholar; it is designed to be used, not studied. And although safeguarding the integrity of both text and annotation has always been a top priority, there is no intention here to offer up this volume as the latest and greatest arbiter of Shakespearean polemics.

Thus, irony reared its impish head, and the hands-off rule of editing was itself amended. But only grudgingly, and only a little. Observe...

- Once in a while it was necessary to shuffle one or more parts of a given speech in order to include all relevant text; entry (1) from *As You Like It*, for example, deftly employs such benign sleight of hand.
- Occasionally, for the sake of clarity or cohesiveness, a bit of another character's line was appropriated for inclusion in the featured monologue. By lending a couple of Nerissa's nondescript lines to Portia in entry (1) from *The Merchant of Venice*, the delightful piece's flow is readily maintained.
- When dealing with verse, a character's own fragmented lines were often linked together in order to keep intact both meter and intended meaning.
- Finally, on very rare occasion it was deemed necessary to add an extraneous word or two to the original text. This sort of liberty was not taken lightly. Rather, it was the last resort of an editor in dire need of a transition, and all such renegade words are clearly marked by brackets.

Yet even with all this regrettable (but necessary) mucking about, the fact remains that fewer than one in ten monologues from *Shakespeare for One* was altered from its standard form in any appreciable way.

Other than the above-mentioned bracketing of extraneous words, no special attention was drawn to departures from the original text. The intention here was not to conceal any rampant editorial license, but merely to facilitate use of the material. The less cluttered a script, the easier it is to work with. Since act, scene, and line information is provided for every entry, it's a simple matter to examine the source text as traditionally presented, should some question arise regarding the piece's integrity.

As to judging where to begin and end each selection, the optimal start and stop points for each speech were usually pretty evident. Keep in mind, though, that the entry and exit lines furnished in *Shakespeare for One* might not be the best available for every conceivable set of circumstances. Feel free to experiment. The idea was to present each entry as completely as possible, thereby allowing each user the opportunity to do their own fine-tuning.

Finally, there is the question of Shakespeare's glorious linguistic idiosyncrasies. Shakespeare would hardly be Shakespeare, of course, without curious constructions such as *to't* and *i'th'*, or compressed verbs like *wond'red* and *o'erwhelm*. And since a prime function of such contractions is to sustain the meter of verse, it seemed far preferable to keep them as they traditionally appear rather than resort to some sort of misbegotten modernization. As to whether or not an extra syllable here or there really matters all that much, well, that's a call for each individual actor to make. It's true that fiddling about with Shakespeare is an endeavor fraught with peril, but the history of theatre is thick with it nonetheless. Fortunately, most situations encountered by the student or auditioning actor are likely to allow for a good deal of flexibility.

Defining Terms

Acting is tricky. Acting Shakespeare is really tricky. Yet even Shakespeare's most daunting and inscrutable passages can be successfully navigated if one is properly prepared for the journey.

An essential element of that preparation is comprehending precisely what, at each and every moment, the author is getting at. There's no denying that Shakespeare's work is marvelously (and oft times maddeningly) elliptical. Even so, solutions are available to most of the tangled webs he weaves. With its comprehensive approach to annotation, *Shakespeare for One* aims to provide the befuddled actor with as many of those solutions as possible.

The definitions and explanations presented in *Shakespeare for One* are based on information gathered from a variety of authoritative sources. In those rare instances when even the collective wisdom of scholars past and present has failed to yield a solution, a consensus best guess, marked with a question mark (?), is offered instead.

Setting the Scene

It goes without saying that the plot-related comments found at the beginning of each chapter and preceding each entry are not offered as stand-ins for actually reading the play. Instead, they are asked to perform two narrowly defined roles: one, set the scene a bit for the uninitiated so they don't have to read an entire play just to test-drive its monologues; and two, gently jog the memories of those who might know a given play but can't quite recall the particulars leading up to the entry at hand.

Should there come a time when more specific plot or character details are required, any of several titles sitting in your local bookstore will do the trick just fine. In fact, the ideal companion piece to *Shakespeare for One* (if you'll permit a bit of cross-promotion) is an outstanding compilation of information and advice entitled *A Guide to Scenes and Monologues from Shakespeare and His Contemporaries*, also published by Heinemann.

But be forewarned that even the best of study guides cannot provide the actor with everything he or she will need in the way of background material. The only way an actor can be fully prepared and can thoroughly appreciate both character and context is to know the source material.

Hamlet got one thing right, anyway: the play *is* the thing.

ALL'S WELL THAT ENDS WELL

When Bertram ventures off to Paris with his companion Parolles, Helena is devastated. Though she's long adored the young Count, the lowborn Helena has always believed him to be unattainable. But things start looking up when, shortly after her own arrival in Paris, Helena cures the King of France of a serious ailment, and by way of reward is granted her one true wish—to have Bertram for her husband.

Though Bertram is duty-bound to do his king's bidding, he clearly resents having to wed Helena. Not long after the wedding ceremony, he spurns his bride and marches off to the wars.

Some time later, Helena learns that her wayward husband is in Florence courting another woman. Before long Helena has concocted an intricate scheme to ensure that Bertram is hers once and for all. After a few unexpected twists and turns, her plan eventually succeeds: Bertram at last sees the error of his ways, he professes to Helena his undying love, and just as promised . . . all's well that ends well.

COUNTESS OF ROSSILLION, mother to Bertram
HELENA, a gentlewoman raised by the Countess

KING OF FRANCE
BERTRAM, Count of Rossillion
PAROLLES, a follower of Bertram

(I)   HELENA   [I.III.191]

SCENE: The Count of Rossillion's palace

{Lowly Helena has long harbored a secret love for the Countess of Rossillion's son,
Bertram. Unfortunately, it would appear that her love is secret no longer. Wilting
under rigorous interrogation by the Countess, Helena is forced to acknowledge
that which, until now, the Countess has only suspected.}

I	I confess here on my knee, before
	High heaven and you, that before you,
	And next unto high heaven, I love your son.
	My friends were poor but honest; so's my love.
5	Be not offended, for it hurts not him
	That he is lov'd of me. I follow him not
	By any token of presumptuous suit,
	Nor would I have him till I do deserve him,
	Yet never know how that desert should be.
10	I know I love in vain, strive against hope;
	Yet in this captious and intenible sieve
	I still pour in the waters of my love
	And lack not to lose still. Thus, Indian-like,
	Religious in mine error, I adore
15	The sun, that looks upon his worshiper,
	But knows of him no more. My dearest madam,
	Let not your hate encounter with my love
	For loving where you do; but if yourself,
	Whose aged honor cites a virtuous youth,
20	Did ever in so true a flame of liking
	Wish chastely and love dearly, that your Dian
	Was both herself and Love, O then give pity
	To her whose state is such that cannot choose
	But lend and give where she is sure to lose;
25	That seeks not to find that her search implies,
	But riddle-like lives sweetly where she dies.

2–3 before ... unto more than (I love) you and second only to   **4 friends**
relatives   **6–7 I ... suit** I do not pursue him in an inappropriately forward
manner (?)   **9 should be** may or will come to be   **10 hope** what can
reasonably be expected   **11 captious** receptive, capacious   **intenible**
incapable of holding   **13 lack ... still** have enough to continually lose more
Indian-like in an idolatrous manner   **14 Religious** scrupulous
17 encounter with fight against, oppose   **19 cites** testifies to, is evidence
of   **20 liking** love   **21 that** so that   **21–22 Dian ... Love** Diana, the virgin
goddess, was both herself and Venus, the goddess of sexual love (i.e., both
chaste and passionate)   **23 state ... that** present state (of mind) is one that

25 that...implies that which she is searching for   **26 riddle-like**
inscrutably (?), with her secret unrevealed (?)

(2)   HELENA   [II.1.100]

SCENE: The King of France's palace

*{Helena attempts to convince the King of France that, despite his doctors' dec-
larations to the contrary, his long-running malady is in fact quite curable.}*

My good lord, on [my father's] bed of death,   1
Many receipts he gave me; chiefly one,
Which, as the dearest issue of his practice,
And of his old experience th' only darling,
He bade me store up, as a triple eye,   5
Safer than mine own two, more dear. I have so;
And, hearing your high Majesty is touch'd
With that malignant cause wherein the honor
Of my dear father's gift stands chief in power,
I come to tender it and my appliance   10
With all bound humbleness.
What I can do can do no hurt to try,
Since you set up your rest 'gainst remedy.
He that of greatest works is finisher
Oft does them by the weakest minister.   15
So holy writ in babes hath judgment shown,
When judges have been babes; great floods have flown
From simple sources, and great seas have dried
When miracles have by the great'st been denied.
Oft expectation fails, and most oft there   20
Where it most promises, and oft it hits
Where hope is coldest and despair most fits.
It is not so with Him that all things knows
As 'tis with us that square our guess by shows;
But most it is presumption in us when   25
The help of heaven we count the act of men.
Dear sir, to my endeavors give consent;
Of heaven, not me, make an experiment.
I am not an impostor that proclaim
Myself against the level of mine aim;   30
But know I think, and think I know most sure,
My art is not past power, nor you past cure.
Ere twice the horses of the sun shall bring
Their fiery torcher his diurnal ring,

35 Ere twice in murk and occidental damp
    Moist Hesperus hath quench'd her sleepy lamp,
    Or four and twenty times the pilot's glass
    Hath told the thievish minutes how they pass,
    What is infirm from your sound parts shall fly;
40 Health shall live free, and sickness freely die.

3 dearest issue most valuable product **4 old** abundant **darling** favorite
5 store up put away for safekeeping **triple** third **6 so** done so
8–9 cause ... power disease against which my dear father's gift (of healing)
is particularly effective **10 tender** offer **appliance** skill in administering it
11 bound dutiful **12 hurt** harm **13 set ... rest** are betting everything
(The phrase comes from a popular game of chance.) **16–17 So ... babes**
(refers to scriptural passages in which babes are better informed than
supposed wise men; see, e.g., Matthew 11:25) **17 flown** (obsolete past
participle of flow) **18 simple** humble, unimposing **18–19 great ...
denied** (probably an allusion to Moses's parting of the Red Sea, with
"great'st" referring to Pharaoh) **21 hits** is fulfilled **24 square ... shows**
base our opinions on outward appearances **26 count** account, regard as
28 make an experiment conduct a trial run **29–30 proclaim ... aim**
boasts of more than I actually intend to do **32 My ... power** the ability that
I claim is not beyond my power **34 torcher ... ring** bearer of light upon
his daily round **35 occidental damp** western (hence, evening) fog or mist
36 Hesperus (the planet Venus, in its role as the evening star) **37 glass**
hourglass **38 told** counted out, revealed **thievish** (because with their
passage they "steal" away time) **40 freely** easily, of its own accord

(3)   HELENA   [III.ii.57]

SCENE: The Count of Rossillion's palace

*{No sooner has Helena married Bertram, the man of her dreams, than she
receives from him a nightmarish letter of repudiation. Clutching the heartless
missive in hand, Helena reflects upon this most sudden and cruel change of
fortune.}*

1   [*Reads from the letter.*] "When thou canst get the ring upon my finger, which
    never shall come off, and show me a child begotten of thy body that I am father
    to, then call me husband; but in such a 'then' I write a 'never.' Till I have no
    wife, I have nothing in France."
5   Nothing in France, until he has no wife!
    Thou shalt have none, Rossillion, none in France;

Then hast thou all again. Poor lord, is 't I
That chase thee from thy country, and expose
Those tender limbs of thine to the event
Of the none-sparing war? And is it I   10
That drive thee from the sportive court, where thou
Wast shot at with fair eyes, to be the mark
Of smoky muskets? O you leaden messengers,
That ride upon the violent speed of fire,
Fly with false aim; move the still-peering air,   15
That sings with piercing; do not touch my lord!
Whoever shoots at him, I set him there;
Whoever charges on his forward breast,
I am the caitiff that do hold him to 't;
And though I kill him not, I am the cause   20
His death was so effected. Better 'twere
I met the ravin lion when he roar'd
With sharp constraint of hunger; better 'twere
That all the miseries which nature owes
Were mine at once. No, come thou home, Rossillion,   25
Whence honor but of danger wins a scar,
As oft it loses all. I will be gone.
My being here it is that holds thee hence.
Shall I stay here to do 't? No, no, although
The air of paradise did fan the house   30
And angels offic'd all. I will be gone,
That pitiful rumor may report my flight
To consolate thine ear. Come, night; end, day!
For with the dark, poor thief, I'll steal away.

6 Rossillion i.e., Bertram (whose title, Count of Rossillion, speaks to the "all" that he shall once again have)   **9 event** consequence (i.e., peril)
10 war (Bertram has gone off "to the wars" to be rid of his unwanted wife.)
11 sportive amorous, passion-laden   **12 to** to (instead)   **mark** target
13 leaden messengers i.e., bullets   **14 fire** the firing of ammunition
15 still-peering (1) always watching (2) looking on unmoved (It is unclear as to just what is meant here—or if "still-peering" is even the proper reading.)
16 sings with piercing whistles with the piercing flight of bullets   **17 set him there** i.e., am responsible for him being there   **19 caitiff** despicable wretch   **hold** force   **21 so effected** thus brought about   **22 ravin** ravenous
23 sharp constraint severe duress   **24 nature owes** human nature possesses   **26 Whence** from the place (i.e., war) where   **26–27 honor . . . all** i.e., honor in the face of danger at best wins a scar, and often loses life itself   **29 do 't** i.e., keep you away from here   **31 offic'd all** performed all household chores   **32 That** so that   **pitiful** compassionate   **33 consolate** console

ANTONY AND CLEOPATRA

Even the considerable charms of Cleopatra cannot detain Antony when word of his wife's death and the threat of an impending civil war compels his return to Rome. Once he's back home, Antony smoothes over a little trouble with his fellow triumvir, Octavius, by marrying Octavius's sister, Octavia. The peace proves short-lived, however, when Antony abandons Rome and his new wife in favor of a return to Egypt and its beguiling Queen of the Nile. War between Antony and Caesar soon follows.

After an initial triumph, Antony's military fortunes soon turn sour when his navy deserts him. Disheartened by defeat, and under the false impression that Cleopatra has died, Antony mortally wounds himself. A short time later he expires in his beloved's arms.

For her part, Cleopatra decides to end things on her own terms rather than succumb to a fate as Octavius's war prize. With loyal attendants by her side, Egypt's queen applies a poisonous snake to her breast and dies.

CLEOPATRA, Queen of Egypt
OCTAVIA, sister to Caesar, wife to Antony
CHARMIAN, attendant to Cleopatra
IRAS, attendant to Cleopatra

MARK ANTONY, a Roman triumvir
OCTAVIUS CAESAR, a Roman triumvir
EROS, friend to Antony

(1)   **CLEOPATRA**   [I.III.18]

SCENE: Cleopatra's palace

{Unrest back home means that Antony must immediately return to Rome, leaving behind both Egypt and his hedonistic lifestyle with Cleopatra. This sudden turn of events does not sit well with the Queen, and she lets Antony know as much.}

Pray you stand farther from me.	1
I know by that same eye there's some good news.	
What, says the married woman you may go?	
Would she had never given you leave to come!	
Let her not say 'tis I that keep you here.	5
I have no power upon you; hers you are.	
O, never was there queen so mightily betray'd!	
Yet at the first I saw the treasons planted.	
Why should I think you can be mine, and true,	
Though you in swearing shake the throned gods,	10
Who have been false to Fulvia? Riotous madness,	
To be entangled with those mouth-made vows,	
Which break themselves in swearing!	
Pray you, seek no color for your going,	
But bid farewell, and go. When you sued staying,	15
Then was the time for words. No going then;	
Eternity was in our lips and eyes,	
Bliss in our brows' bent; none our parts so poor	
But was a race of heaven. They are so still,	
Or thou, the greatest soldier of the world,	20
Art turn'd the greatest liar.	

3 married woman i.e., Fulvia, Antony's wife   **11 Who** you who
12 mouth-made i.e., spoken but not truly felt, insincere   **13 break...**
swearing are broken even as they're being sworn   **14 color** pretense
15 sued staying begged to stay   **17 our** i.e., my (Cleopatra is employing
the royal plural)   **18 bent** arch   **parts** features, qualities   **19 a...heaven**
of heavenly origin

(2)   CLEOPATRA   [V.II.76]

SCENE: Cleopatra's monument

{Even as her world falls in around her, Cleopatra finds a serene moment in which to muse upon the singular qualities of her fallen lover, Mark Antony.}

1   I dreamt there was an Emperor Antony.
    O, such another sleep, that I might see
    But such another man!
    His face was as the heav'ns, and therein stuck
5   A sun and moon, which kept their course, and lighted
    The little O, the earth.
    His legs bestrid the ocean, his rear'd arm
    Crested the world, his voice was propertied
    As all the tuned spheres, and that to friends;
10   But when he meant to quail and shake the orb,
    He was as rattling thunder. For his bounty,
    There was no winter in 't; an autumn it was
    That grew the more by reaping. His delights
    Were dolphin-like; they show'd his back above
15   The element they liv'd in. In his livery
    Walk'd crowns and crownets; realms and islands were
    As plates dropp'd from his pocket. Think you there was,
    Or might be, such a man as this I dreamt of?
    If there be nor ever were one such,
20   It's past the size of dreaming. Nature wants stuff
    To vie strange forms with fancy; yet t' imagine
    An Antony were nature's piece 'gainst fancy,
    Condemning shadows quite.

7 bestrid straddled   **8 Crested** topped, served as a crest to (A raised arm was a common image in heraldry.)   **8–9 propertied...friends** endowed with the same harmonious quality apparent in the motion of the heavenly bodies, whenever he spoke to his friends   **10 quail** terrify   **orb** world   **11 bounty** generosity, munificence   **13–15 His...in** i.e., his taste in pleasures rose above the common and ordinary, just as the dolphin is able to rise above its element, the sea   **15 livery** retinue (and thus wearing Antony's livery)   **16 crowns and crownets** kings and princes   **17 plates** silver coins   **18 might** could   **19 If...were** i.e., whether or not there is or ever was   **20 It's...dreaming** no dream can match my image of him   **20–21 Nature...fancy** i.e., nature lacks what it takes to compete with one's imagination in the creation of such remarkable forms   **22 piece 'gainst fancy** masterpiece in its competition with the imagination   **23 Condemning shadows** discrediting mere fantasies

(3)   **CLEOPATRA**   [V.II.280]

SCENE: Cleopatra's monument

{With the aid of her attendants Iras and Charmian, the Queen dons her royal garb one last time, resolved to conclude matters on her own terms rather than face becoming a trophy to the victorious Octavius.}

Give me my robe, put on my crown; I have   1
Immortal longings in me. Now no more
The juice of Egypt's grape shall moist this lip.
Yare, yare, good Iras; quick. Methinks I hear
Antony call; I see him rouse himself   5
To praise my noble act. I hear him mock
The luck of Caesar, which the gods give men
To excuse their after wrath. Husband, I come!
Now to that name my courage prove my title!
I am fire and air; my other elements   10
I give to baser life. Come, thou mortal wretch,
[*She applies an asp to her breast.*]
With thy sharp teeth this knot intrinsicate
Of life at once untie. Poor venomous fool,
Be angry, and dispatch. O, couldst thou speak,   15
That I might hear thee call great Caesar ass
Unpolicied! Peace, peace [Charmian]!
Dost thou not see my baby at my breast,
That sucks the nurse asleep?
As sweet as balm, as soft as air, as gentle—   20
O Antony!—Nay, I will take thee too.
[*Applies another asp on to her arm.*]
What should I stay—
[*She dies.*]

2 Immortal longings longings for the afterlife   **4 Yare** quick   **8 their** i.e., the gods **after wrath** wrath directed at those who have been fortunate **9 title** right   **10 other elements** i.e., earth and water (Ancient philosophy held that all material bodies were composed of the same four basic substances; earth, water, air, and fire.)   **11 baser** i.e., mortal **mortal wretch** deadly creature ("wretch" is used here as a term of endearment) **13 intrinsicate** intricate   **14 fool** (used here as a term of endearment) **15 dispatch** kill   **17 Unpolicied** outwitted   **23 What** for what reason

ALTERNATE
Cleopatra   [V.ii.150–175]

AS YOU LIKE IT

Orlando, fearing for his life and fed up with his brother Oliver's neglectful guardianship, decides to seek his fortune elsewhere. Accompanied by his old friend and servant, Adam, he arrives in the Forest of Arden and joins the company of Duke Senior, who's been living in banishment since his evil brother, Frederick, usurped his title.

When Orlando's beloved Rosalind is likewise banished by Frederick, she disguises herself as a boy and, accompanied her cousin, Celia, and Touchstone the fool, she strikes out in search of her father, Duke Senior. When she and Orlando happen to meet in the forest, Rosalind decides to have some fun with the fact that he cannot see through her disguise by offering to school the lovesick lad on the finer points of romance.

Elsewhere in the forest, Silvius the shepherd is having no luck at all in wooing the affections of a local maiden named Phebe. After Rosalind overhears Phebe's heartless rebuff of poor Silvius, she steps in to severely upbraid the maid for her cruelty—and, by doing so, induces Phebe to fall in love with her.

Eventually, everything turns out swell: Rosalind drops her disguise and reunites with Orlando, Phebe makes up with Silvius, a repentant Oliver shows up just in time to pair off with Celia, a similarly reformed Frederick restores to Duke Senior his rightful position, and even Touchstone finds love as marriage and merriment abound.

ROSALIND, daughter to Duke Senior
CELIA, daughter to Duke Frederick, cousin to Rosalind
PHEBE, a shepherdess

DUKE SENIOR, living in banishment
DUKE FREDERICK, brother to Duke Senior
OLIVER, in love with Rosalind
ORLANDO, brother to Orlando
ADAM, servant to Oliver
TOUCHSTONE, a professional fool
SILVIUS, a shepherd, in love with Phebe

(1)   CELIA   [I.III.90]

SCENE: Duke Frederick's palace

{Moments ago, Duke Frederick abruptly banished Rosalind from his court, and then stormed away. Rosalind's cousin, Celia, is so distraught over this unfortunate development that one would think it was she who was suddenly leaving home. Which, if she has her way...}

O my poor Rosalind, whither wilt thou go?   I
Wilt thou change fathers? If [thou art] a traitor,
Why so am I. We still have slept together,
Rose at an instant, learn'd, play'd, eat together,
And wheresoe'er we went, like Juno's swans,   5
Still we went coupled and inseparable.
Shall we be sund'red? Shall we part, sweet girl?
No, let my father seek another heir.
Therefore devise with me how we may fly,
Whither to go, and what to bear with us.   10
And do not seek to take your change upon you,
To bear your griefs yourself and leave me out;
For, by this heaven, now at our sorrows pale,
Say what thou canst, I'll go along with thee.
[We'll] seek my uncle in the forest of Arden.   15
I'll put myself in poor and mean attire
And with a kind of umber smirch my face;
The like you do. So shall we pass along
And never stir assailants. Let's away,
And get our jewels and our wealth together,   20
Devise the fittest time and safest way
To hide us from pursuit that will be made
After my flight. Now go we in content
To liberty, and not to banishment.

2 traitor (The Duke justified his banishment of Rosalind by claiming that she was, or soon would become, a traitor.) **3 still** always **4 eat** eaten
5 Juno's swans (Actually it was Venus, and not Juno, who had an affinity for swans.) **7 sund'red** separated **11 change** change of fortune and circumstances **13 pale** cheerless **15 uncle** (referring to Duke Senior)
16 mean lowly, base **17 umber** brown pigment **18 The...do** you do the same **19 stir** arouse, attract the attention of **23 content** contentment

(2)   ROSALIND   [III.ii.370]

SCENE: The Forest of Arden

{Orlando is hopelessly infatuated with Rosalind. Rosalind is taken with Orlando as well, but it's the maid's more playful side that shows itself here. Disguised as a boy, she rolls out an unlikely and elaborate plan to test the earnestness of her lover's suit.}

1   [My uncle] taught me how to know a man in love, in which cage of rushes I am
       sure you are not a prisoner. His marks are a lean cheek, which you have not; a
       blue eye and sunken, which you have not; an unquestionable spirit, which you
       have not; a beard neglected, which you have not—but I pardon you for that, for
5   simply your having in beard is a younger brother's revenue. Then your hose
       should be ungarter'd, your bonnet unbanded, your sleeve unbutton'd, your
       shoe untied, and everything about you demonstrating a careless desolation.
       But you are no such man; you are rather point-device in your accouterments,
       as loving yourself, than seeming the lover of any other. [Ere you] could make
10   me believe you love, you may as soon make her that you love believe it, which
       I warrant she is apter to do than to confess she does. That is one of the points
       in the which women still give the lie to their consciences. [Yet,] there is a man
       haunts the forest, that abuses our young plants with carving "Rosalind" on their
       barks, hangs odes upon hawthorns, and elegies upon brambles; all, forsooth,
15   deifying the name of Rosalind. In good sooth, are you he that hangs these
       verses on the trees, wherein Rosalind is so admired? Are you so much in love
       as your rhymes speak? [For] love is merely a madness, and, I tell you, deserves
       as well a dark house and a whip as madmen do; and the reason why they are
       not so punish'd and cur'd is that the lunacy is so ordinary that the whippers
20   are in love too. Yet I profess curing it by counsel; [and once] did so in this
       manner. The fancy-monger was to imagine me his love, his mistress; and I set
       him every day to woo me. At which time would I, being but a moonish youth,
       grieve, be effeminate, changeable, longing and liking, proud, fantastical, apish,
       shallow, inconstant, full of tears, full of smiles; for every passion something and
25   for no passion truly anything, as boys and women are for the most part cattle
       of this color; would now like him, now loathe him; then entertain him, then
       forswear him; now weep for him, then spit at him; that I drave my suitor from
       his mad humor of love to a living humor of madness, which was, to forswear
       the full stream of the world and to live in a nook merely monastic. And thus
30   I cur'd him; and this way will I take upon me to wash your liver as clean as a
       sound sheep's heart, that there shall not be one spot of love in 't. I would cure
       you, if you would but call me Rosalind, and come every day to my cote and
       woo me. Go with me to it, and I'll show it you; and by the way you shall tell
       me where in the forest you live. Will you go?

I know recognize, distinguish **cage of rushes** i.e., flimsy prison from which it is easy to escape **3 blue eye** dark circles (caused by crying and lack of sleep) **5 simply** frankly **having...revenue** what you have in the way of a beard is as small as a younger brother's inheritance (The younger sons in a family traditionally received small inheritances.) **6 bonnet unbanded** hat should have no band around it (which was considered a sloppy and unseemly way of wearing one) **8 point-device** very precise, correct **12 still** continually **give...to** belie, misrepresent **consciences** innermost thoughts, true emotions **13 haunts** who haunts **15 In good sooth** truthfully **18 dark...whip** (Such being typical of the treatment dispensed to the mentally ill in that day and age.) **they** (referring to those in love) **19 ordinary** commonplace **20 profess** declare myself an expert in **21 fancy-monger** peddler of love **22 moonish** fickle, constantly changing (like the moon) **23 proud** vain **fantastical** capricious **apish** affected in manner, silly **27 drave** drove **28 mad...madness** fantasy of love to a state of literal madness **29 nook** protected creek (used figuratively, in conjunction with the "full stream" imagery) **merely monastic** utterly reclusive **30 liver** (The liver was thought by some to be the source of a person's love and passion.) **32 cote** cottage **33 by** along

(3)   **ROSALIND**   [III.v.34]

SCENE: The Forest of Arden

{Rosalind has been lurking nearby in the bushes, eavesdropping on Phebe's cruel rebuff of poor Silvius. Having overheard all she can stand, Rosalind—still disguised as a boy—finally emerges from cover and confronts the abusive maid.}

I pray you, who might be your mother,   1
That you insult, exult, and all at once,
Over the wretched? What though you have no beauty—
As, by faith, I see no more in you
Than without candle may go dark to bed—   5
Must you therefore be proud and pitiless?
Why, what means this? Why do you look on me?
I see no more in you than in the ordinary
Of nature's sale-work. 'Od's my little life,
I think she means to tangle my eyes too!   10
No, faith, proud mistress, hope not after it.
'Tis not your inky brows, your black silk hair,

Your bugle eyeballs, nor your cheek of cream
That can entame my spirits to your worship.
15   You foolish shepherd, wherefore do you follow her,
Like foggy south, puffing with wind and rain?
You are a thousand times a properer man
Than she a woman. 'Tis such fools as you
That makes the world full of ill-favor'd children.
20   'Tis not her glass, but you, that flatters her,
And out of you she sees herself more proper
Than any of her lineaments can show her.
But, mistress, know yourself. Down on your knees,
And thank heaven, fasting, for a good man's love;
25   For I must tell you friendly in your ear,
Sell when you can, you are not for all markets.
Cry the man mercy; love him, take his offer.
Foul is most foul, being foul to be a scoffer.
So take her to thee, shepherd. Fare you well.

3 wretched pitiable   **4 by faith** in truth   **4–5 I . . . bed** i.e., I see no
beauty in you so shining that it would light your way to bed   **7 this** i.e.,
Phebe's staring (It seems that, with her unabashed leering, Phebe is already
betraying her infatuation with Rosalind.)   **9 sale-work** ready-made goods
(and thus goods of commonplace, or "ordinary," quality)   **'Od's** God save
10 tangle entrap   **11 faith** by my faith (a mild oath)   **13 bugle eyeballs**
eyes like black, shiny beads   **14 entame** dominate, subdue   **your worship**
worship of you   **16 south** south wind (which in England brings fog and rain)
wind and rain (referring to Silvius's sighs and tears)   **17 properer** more
handsome   **19 ill-favor'd** ugly   **20 glass** looking glass   **25 friendly** as your
friend   **27 Cry . . . mercy** beg the man's pardon   **28 Foul . . . scoffer**
unseemliness (in a woman) is even more repulsive when (she) scoffs at an
offer of love

(4)   PHEBE   [III.v.92]

SCENE: The Forest of Arden

*{Even as Rosalind berated Phebe for her heartless treatment of Silvius (see
preceding entry), Phebe grew completely infatuated with her still-in-disguise
scorner. Now that Rosalind has gone, Phebe realizes she simply must come up
with a pretext for seeing the "lad" again, and so turns to the woeful Silvius for
assistance.}*

Silvius, the time was that I hated thee;   1
And yet it is not that I bear thee love.
But since that thou canst talk of love so well,
Thy company, which erst was irksome to me,
I will endure, and I'll employ thee too.   5
But do not look for further recompense
Than thine own gladness that thou art employ'd.
Know'st thou the youth that spoke to me erewhile?
Think not I love him, though I ask for him;
'Tis but a peevish boy; yet he talks well.   10
But what care I for words? Yet words do well
When he that speaks them pleases those that hear.
It is a pretty youth—not very pretty—
But, sure, he's proud, and yet his pride becomes him.
He'll make a proper man. The best thing in him   15
Is his complexion; and, faster than his tongue
Did make offense, his eye did heal it up.
He is not very tall; yet for his years he's tall.
His leg is but so so; and yet 'tis well.
There was a pretty redness in his lip,   20
A little riper and more lusty red
Than that mix'd in his cheek; 'twas just the difference
Betwixt the constant red and mingled damask.
There be some women, Silvius, had they mark'd him
In parcels as I did, would have gone near   25
To fall in love with him; but, for my part,
I love him not nor hate him not; and yet
I have more cause to hate him than to love him.
For what had he to do to chide at me?
He said mine eyes were black and my hair black;   30
And, now I am rememb'red, scorn'd at me.
I marvel why I answer'd not again.
But that's all one; omittance is no quittance.
I'll write to him a very taunting letter,
And thou shalt bear it. I will write it straight;   35
The matter's in my head and in my heart.
I will be bitter with him and passing short.
Go with me, Silvius.

2 yet...not the time has still not come   **4 erst** erstwhile, formerly
8 erewhile earlier on   **17 eye** appearance   **21 lusty** vigorous
23 constant uniform   **mingled damask** red and white mixed, as in the
color of the damask rose   **25 In parcels** in detail, piece by piece
25–26 gone...fall come close to falling   **29 what...do** what business
was it of his   **31 I am rememb'red** that I recall   **33 all one** no matter

omittance . . . quittance not answering him now doesn't mean that I may not do so later   **35 straight** immediately   **37 passing short** very abrupt, extremely rude

(5)   ROSALIND   [EPILOGUE]

{Play is done, save for Rosalind's gentle goodbye.}

1   It is not the fashion to see the lady the epilogue; but it is no more unhandsome than to see the lord the prologue. If it be true that good wine needs no bush, 'tis true that a good play needs no epilogue. Yet to good wine they do use good bushes, and good plays prove the better by the help of good epilogues.

5   What a case am I in then, that am neither a good epilogue nor cannot insinuate with you in the behalf of a good play! I am not furnish'd like a beggar, therefore to beg will not become me. My way is to conjure you, and I'll begin with the women. I charge you, O women, for the love you bear to men, to like as much of this play as please you; and I charge you, O men, for the love you bear

10   to women—as I perceive by your simp'ring, none of you hates them—that between you and the women the play may please. If I were a woman I would kiss as many of you as had beards that pleas'd me, complexions that lik'd me, and breaths that I defied not; and, I am sure, as many as have good beards or good faces, or sweet breaths will, for my kind offer, when I make curtsy, bid

15   me farewell.

1 unhandsome improper, unbecoming   **2 bush** (Signs out front of a tavern or wine shop typically featured an ivy bush.)   **5 case** predicament
insinuate ingratiate myself   **6 furnish'd** dressed, decked out   **7 conjure** entreat solemnly, implore   **11 If . . . woman** (In Shakespeare's time, female characters were portrayed by boys.)   **12 lik'd** pleased   **13 defied** disliked
14–15 bid me farewell i.e., applaud me

THE COMEDY OF ERRORS

Twenty-three years ago, there was a ship that foundered in a storm. Among the ship's passengers tossed into the raging sea were a merchant, his wife, their twin baby boys (both named Antipholus), and another set of infant twins (both named Dromio) being raised by them.

Fortunately, everyone was rescued; unfortunately, not by the same rescue parties. As things turned out, the merchant, one Antipholus, and one Dromio were taken to Syracuse, while the merchant's wife, the other Antipholus, and the other Dromio ended up in the city of Ephesus.

After turning eighteen, the pair of twins from Syracuse set out in search of their long-lost brothers, and five years into their quest finally arrive in Ephesus. Because no one realizes that there are now two Antipholuses and two Dromios in town, a series of mistaken identifications and general mayhem ensue. Eventually, of course, everything is set right and the long-separated families are reunited.

ADRIANA, wife to Antipholus of Ephesus
LUCIANA, sister to Adriana

ANTIPHOLUS OF EPHESUS, twin brother to Antipholus of Syracuse

ANTIPHOLUS OF SYRACUSE, twin brother to Antipholus of Ephesus, in love with Luciana

DROMIO OF EPHESUS, twin brother to Dromio of Syracuse, servant to Antipholus of Ephesus

DROMIO OF SYRACUSE, twin brother to Dromio of Ephesus, servant to Antipholus of Syracuse

(1)   ADRIANA   [II.1.87]

SCENE: Before the house of Antipholus of Ephesus

{Adriana's husband has reportedly denied any knowledge of their home or marriage, and Adriana is at a loss to explain why. She suspects, however, that Antipholus has found greener pastures in which to graze.}

1   [Must] I at home starve for a merry look?
     Hath homely age th' alluring beauty took
     From my poor cheek? Then he hath wasted it.
     Are my discourses dull? Barren my wit?
5   If voluble and sharp discourse be marr'd,
     Unkindness blunts it more than marble hard.
     Do their gay vestments his affections bait?
     That's not my fault; he's master of my state.
     What ruins are in me that can be found,
10   By him not ruin'd? Then is he the ground
     Of my defeatures. My decayed fair
     A sunny look of his would soon repair.
     But, too unruly deer, he breaks the pale
     And feeds from home; poor I am but his stale.
15   I know his eye doth homage otherwhere,
     Or else what lets it but he would be here?
     Sister, you know he promis'd me a chain;
     Would that alone, alone he would detain,
     So he would keep fair quarter with his bed!
20   I see the jewel best enameled
     Will lose his beauty; yet the gold bides still
     That others touch, and often touching will
     Wear gold; and no man that hath a name,
     By falsehood and corruption doth it shame.
25   Since that my beauty cannot please his eye,
     I'll weep what's left away, and weeping die.

2 age i.e., old age   **3 wasted it** (1) laid it to waste (2) squandered it
4 discourses conversations   **Barren** slow, dull   **5 voluble** well-spoken,
fluent   **sharp** witty   **7 affections** passions   **bait** entice   **8 state** outward
estate, i.e., clothes   **10 ground** cause   **11 defeatures** disrepair   **decayed**
vanished, perished   **fair** beauty   **13 pale** fence   **14 from** away from   **stale**
laughingstock (with a play on the common sense of "stale," i.e., tiresome, old
hat)   **15 otherwhere** elsewhere   **16 lets...here** prevents him from being
here   **18 Would...detain** if only he would withhold merely that token of
his love   **19 So** provided   **keep...with** remain faithful to   **bed** marriage
bed   **20–24 I...shame** (A difficult passage that's probably corrupt, the

sense here seems to be that Adriana's beauty, like a fine enameled jewel, will tarnish through neglect. A setting of gold, on the other hand, will retain its luster despite much use—in the same way a man of solid reputation will retain his good name even while subjecting it to the wear and tear of infidelity and deception.)

(2) **ADRIANA** [II.ii.110]

SCENE: A street in Ephesus

{Adriana is at a loss to explain why her husband, Antipholus, has suddenly become so contrary, even to the point of denying that the two of them are man and wife. What she fails to realize, unfortunately, is that she's addressing the "wrong" Antipholus. The man before her is actually her husband's long-lost identical twin brother, not the Antipholus she knows and loves.}

Ay, ay, Antipholus, look strange and frown.   1
Some other mistress hath thy sweet aspects;
I am not Adriana nor thy wife.
The time was once when thou unurg'd wouldst vow
That never words were music to thine ear,   5
That never object pleasing in thine eye,
That never touch well welcome to thy hand,
That never meat sweet-savor'd in thy taste,
Unless I spake, or look'd, or touch'd, or carv'd to thee.
How comes it now, my husband, O, how comes it,   10
That thou art thus estranged from thyself?
Thyself I call it, being strange to me,
That, undividable incorporate,
Am better than thy dear self's better part.
Ah, do not tear away thyself from me!   15
For know, my love, as easy mayst thou fall
A drop of water in the breaking gulf
And take unmingled thence that drop again,
Without addition or diminishing,
As take from me thyself and not me too.   20
How dearly would it touch thee to the quick,
Shouldst thou but hear I were licentious,
And that this body, consecrate to thee,
By ruffian lust should be contaminate!
Wouldst thou not spit at me, and spurn at me,   25
And hurl the name of husband in my face,

And tear the stain'd skin off my harlot-brow,
And from my false hand cut the wedding-ring,
And break it with a deep-divorcing vow?
30   I know thou canst, and therefore see thou do it.
I am possess'd with an adulterate blot;
My blood is mingled with the crime of lust:
For if we two be one and thou play false,
I do digest the poison of thy flesh,
35   Being strumpeted by thy contagion.
Keep then fair league and truce with thy true bed;
I live distain'd, thou undishonored.

1 strange distant, estranged   **2 aspects** looks, glances   **13 undividable incorporate** indivisibly united with (you)   **14 better than** more than **16 fall** let fall   **17 breaking gulf** swirling whirlpool   **18 thence** from there **21 dearly** deeply   **23 consecrate** dedicated   **24 contaminate** contaminated   **25 spurn at** spurn   **29 deep** profoundly, intensely **35 strumpeted** made a harlot, defiled   **contagion** poisonous influence **36 fair league** a virtuous partnership   **37 distain'd** untarnished (by your corruption)

(3)   LUCIANA   [III.ii.1]

SCENE: Before the house of Antipholus of Ephesus

{Antipholus of Syracuse has fallen in love with Luciana. But Luciana will have none of his amorous intentions, believing as she does that this is the same Antipholus (i.e., of Ephesus) who is married to her sister, Adriana.}

1   And may it be that you have quite forgot
A husband's office? Shall, Antipholus,
Even in the spring of love, thy love-springs rot?
Shall love, in building, grow so ruinous?
5   If you did wed my sister for her wealth,
Then for her wealth's sake use her with more kindness;
Or if you like elsewhere, do it by stealth;
Muffle your false love with some show of blindness.
Let not my sister read it in your eye;
10   Be not thy tongue thy own shame's orator;
Look sweet, speak fair, become disloyalty;
Apparel vice like virtue's harbinger.
Bear a fair presence, though your heart be tainted;
Teach sin the carriage of a holy saint;

Be secret-false. What need she be acquainted?   15
What simple thief brags of his own attaint?
'Tis double wrong, to truant with your bed
And let her read it in thy looks at board.
Shame hath a bastard fame, well managed;
Ill deeds is doubled with an evil word.   20
Alas, poor women! Make us but believe,
Being compact of credit, that you love us;
Though others have the arm, show us the sleeve;
We in your motion turn, and you may move us.
Then, gentle brother, get you in again.   25
Comfort my sister, cheer her, call her wife.
'Tis holy sport to be a little vain,
When the sweet breath of flattery conquers strife.

2 office duty, function **3 love-springs** tender beginnings of love
4 ruinous decayed **7 like elsewhere** i.e., choose to lavish affection on
someone else **8 Muffle** cover up **blindness** concealment, subterfuge
11 fair kindly **become disloyalty** bear infidelity with grace **14 carriage**
demeanor **15 secret-false** secretly unfaithful **What...acquainted?**
Why must she be made aware (of your infidelity)? **16 simple thief** thief is
so stupid that he **attaint** disgrace **17 truant with** be unfaithful to
18 board the (dinner) table **19 bastard** artificial, counterfeit **well**
managed when skillfully handled **22 compact of credit** made up of
gullibility **24 We...turn** we are governed by you **27 vain** deceitful

ALTERNATE
Adriana [V.i.136]

CORIOLANUS

Though roundly criticized for his arrogance and lack of compassion in a time of famine, Coriolanus is nonetheless the man the people turn to when Rome comes under the threat of an attack by the Volscian army. His courageous leadership brings victory to the Romans, for which he is duly praised. But his contemptuous ways soon incite the masses (and some jealous tribunes) against him, and before long he is banished.

Looking to exact some revenge, Coriolanus offers to join his former enemy, the Volscian general Aufidius, in an assault upon Rome. Only a last-minute plea by Coriolanus's mother, Volumnia, persuades Coriolanus to preempt the attack and instead arrange a truce between the two armies.

When he too grows jealous of Coriolanus's rising popularity, Aufidius decries the Roman's efforts for peace as a betrayal of the Volscian people. Aufidius's propaganda soon bears fruit: Coriolanus is ultimately murdered at the behest of a mob and at the hands of Aufidius's assassins.

VOLUMNIA, mother to Coriolanus

CORIOLANUS, a Roman statesman and general
MENENIUS AGRIPPA, friend to Coriolanus
TULLUS AUFIDIUS, general of the Volscians

(1)   **VOLUMNIA**   **[III.ii.28]**

SCENE: Coriolanus's house

{Earlier, while caught up in one of his customary fits of rage, Coriolanus said
and did some rather inflammatory things before a clutch of senators, patricians,
and the like. Now it falls to Volumnia to convince her son that he must, for his
own welfare, humble himself and beg forgiveness for his rash behavior.}

Pray be counsel'd.	1
I have a heart as little apt as yours,	
But yet a brain that leads my use of anger	
To better vantage. You are too absolute;	
Though therein you can never be too noble,	5
But when extremities speak. I have heard you say	
Honor and policy, like unsever'd friends,	
I' th' war do grow together. Grant that, and tell me	
In peace what each of them by th' other lose	
That they combine not there.	10
If it be honor in your wars to seem	
The same you are not, which, for your best ends,	
You adopt your policy, how is it less or worse	
That it shall hold companionship in peace	
With honor, as in war, since that to both	15
It stands in like request? It lies you on to speak	
To th' people, not by your own instruction,	
Nor by th' matter which your heart prompts you,	
But with such words that are but roted in	
Your tongue, though but bastards and syllables	20
Of no allowance to your bosom's truth.	
Now, this no more dishonors you at all	
Than to take in a town with gentle words,	
Which else would put you to your fortune and	
The hazard of much blood.	25
I would dissemble with my nature where	
My fortunes and my friends at stake requir'd	
I should do so in honor. I am in this	
Your wife, your son, these senators, the nobles;	
And you will rather show our general louts	30
How you can frown, than spend a fawn upon 'em	
For the inheritance of their loves and safeguard	
Of what that want might ruin. I prithee, my son,	
Go to them, with this bonnet in thy hand,	
And thus far having stretch'd it—here be with them—	35
Thy knee bussing the stones; for in such business	

Action is eloquence, and the eyes of th' ignorant
More learned than the ears; waving thy head,
Which often thus correcting thy stout heart,
40   Now humble as the ripest mulberry
That will not hold the handling. Or say to them
Thou art their soldier, and, being bred in broils,
Hast not the soft way which, thou dost confess,
Were fit for thee to use as they to claim,
45   In asking their good loves, but thou wilt frame
Thyself, forsooth, hereafter theirs, so far
As thou hast power and person. Prithee now,
Go, and be rul'd; although I know thou hadst rather
Follow thine enemy in a fiery gulf
50   Than flatter him in a bower.

2 apt submissive, docile   **4 absolute** unyielding   **6 extremities speak** an extreme situation demands   **7 policy** shrewd maneuvering **unsever'd** inseparable   **10 combine** unite, ally   **12 The same** that which   **13 your** as your   **16 like request** equal demand **lies you on** is your obligation **18 prompts** suggests (to)   **19 roted** learned by rote   **21 Of...to** unsanctioned by   **23 take in** capture   **24 put...fortune** i.e., oblige you to do battle   **25 hazard** putting at risk   **26 dissemble...nature** disguise my true feelings   **28 I...this** in this (view) I represent   **30 general** common   **31 fawn** act of self-abasement   **32 inheritance** acquisition **33 want** lack (i.e., of their loves)   **prithee** pray thee, beg of you **34 this...hand** i.e., hat in hand (as a gesture of respect)   **35 And... them** and holding (your hat) out like this—do it this way for them (Volumnia demonstrates the gesture for him)   **36 bussing** kissing   **38 learned** perceptive, accomplished **waving** bowing   **39 correcting** disciplining **stout** proud   **40 humble as** i.e., is as soft and pliant as   **41 hold the** withstand   **42 broils** battles   **44 fit** as fit **they** for them **claim** demand (of you)   **45 frame** shape, form   **46 theirs** according to their wishes **46–47 so...person** so far as it is within your power to do so   **49 in** into **50 bower** arbor or other garden-like retreat

(2)   VOLUMNIA   [V.iii.87]

SCENE: Coriolanus's tent in the Volscian camp

{With a Volscian attack on Rome now imminent, Volumnia has come here to the enemy camp accompanied by Coriolanus's wife, son, and others. Upon being presented to her son (who's been helping the Volscians since his banishment from Rome), Volumnia pulls out all the stops in a last-ditch effort to save her city.}

[This speech can be abbreviated in a number of ways; effective alternate
end points include lines 37, 54 and 71.]

You have said you will not grant us anything;   1
For we have nothing else to ask but that
Which you deny already. Yet we will ask,
That, if you fail in our request, the blame
May hang upon your hardness. Therefore hear us.   5
Should we be silent and not speak, our raiment
And state of bodies would bewray what life
We have led since thy exile. Think with thyself
How more unfortunate than all living women
Are we come hither; since that thy sight, which should   10
Make our eyes flow with joy, hearts dance with comforts,
Constrains them weep and shake with fear and sorrow,
Making the mother, wife, and child to see
The son, the husband, and the father tearing
His country's bowels out. And to poor we   15
Thine enmity's most capital. Thou barr'st us
Our prayers to the gods, which is a comfort
That all but we enjoy; for how can we,
Alas, how can we for our country pray,
Whereto we are bound, together with thy victory,   20
Whereto we are bound? Alack, or we must lose
The country, our dear nurse, or else thy person,
Our comfort in the country. We must find
An evident calamity, though we had
Our wish, which side should win; for either thou   25
Must as a foreign recreant be led
With manacles through our streets, or else
Triumphantly tread on thy country's ruin,
And bear the palm for having bravely shed
Thy wife and children's blood. For myself, son,   30
I purpose not to wait on fortune till
These wars determine. If I cannot persuade thee
Rather to show a noble grace to both parts
Than seek the end of one, thou shalt no sooner
March to assault thy country than to tread—   35
Trust to 't, thou shalt not—on thy mother's womb
That brought thee to this world.
If it were so that our request did tend
To save the Romans, thereby to destroy
The Volsces whom you serve, you might condemn us   40
As poisonous of your honor. No, our suit
Is that you reconcile them, while the Volsces

BOONE COUNTY
322 8191

May say, "This mercy we have show'd," the Romans,
"This we receiv'd," and each in either side
45   Give the all-hail to thee, and cry, "Be blest
For making up this peace!" Thou know'st, great son,
The end of war's uncertain; but this certain,
That, if thou conquer Rome, the benefit
Which thou shalt thereby reap is such a name
50   Whose repetition will be dogg'd with curses,
Whose chronicle thus writ: "The man was noble,
But with his last attempt he wip'd it out,
Destroy'd his country, and his name remains
To th' ensuing age abhorr'd." Speak to me, son.
55   Thou hast affected the fine strains of honor,
To imitate the graces of the gods;
To tear with thunder the wide cheeks o' th' air,
And yet to charge thy sulphur with a bolt
That should but rive an oak. Why dost not speak?
60   Think'st thou it honorable for a nobleman
Still to remember wrongs? There's no man in the world
More bound to 's mother, yet here he lets me prate
Like one i' th' stocks.—Thou hast never in thy life
Show'd thy dear mother any courtesy,
65   When she, poor hen, fond of no second brood,
Has cluck'd thee to the wars and safely home,
Loaden with honor. Say my request's unjust,
And spurn me back; but if it be not so,
Thou art not honest, and the gods will plague thee
70   That thou restrain'st from me the duty which
To a mother's part belongs.—He turns away.
Down, ladies! Let us shame him with our knees.
To his surname Coriolanus 'longs more pride
Than pity to our prayers. Down! [*She kneels.*] An end;
75   This is the last. So we will home to Rome,
And die among our neighbors. Come, let us go.
This fellow had a Volscian to his mother;
His wife is in Corioles, and this child
Like him by chance.—Yet give us our dispatch.
80   I am hush'd until our city be afire,
And then I'll speak a little.

4 fail in refuse   **6 Should we** even if we should   **7 bewray** betray, reveal
10 come to come   **11 comforts** delight, gladness   **12 Constrains them**
forces them (to)   **16 capital** deadly   **20 bound** under obligation   **21 or**
either   **24 evident** certain   **25 which** whichever   **26 recreant** villain,
traitor   **29 bear the palm** (an act emblematic of victory)   **31 purpose**

intend, am resolved   **32 determine** come to an end   **33 grace** mercy
parts sides, parties   **47 this** this much is   **51 chronicle** history (will be)
52 attempt enterprise, undertaking   **it** i.e., his nobility   **55 affected**
aspired to, cherished   **strains** qualities   **58 charge** load   **sulphur** lightning
59 but . . . oak i.e., cause only inconsequential damage (The image Volumnia
invokes here is one of Coriolanus striving to emulate the gods in judiciously
exercising his awesome power.)   **61 Still** forever   **62 prate** prattle, babble
65 When while   **fond** desirous   **67 Loaden** laden   **69 honest** honorable
70 restrain'st withhold   **72 knees** i.e., kneeling   **73 'longs** belongs
74 An end no more   **77 This fellow** i.e., Coriolanus   **to** for   **78 this
child** i.e., Coriolanus's son   **79 Like him by** resembles him only by mere
dispatch leave to go

ALTERNATE
Volumnia   [I.iii.1–25]

CYMBELINE

Cymbeline simply would not stand for his daughter Imogen's secret marriage to Posthumus, and so he had the poor lad banished. Landing on his feet in Rome, Posthumus wagers with a local scoundrel named Iachimo that his beloved Imogen cannot be corrupted. Though Iachimo fails miserably in his attempt to seduce Imogen, he returns from Britain with enough misleading evidence to convince Posthumus otherwise.

Incensed by his wife's apparent betrayal, Posthumus dashes off a letter to Pisanio (his manservant back in Britain) that instructs him to murder Imogen. Pisanio, however, is unable to do his master's bidding. Instead, he persuades Imogen to make her way to Rome—for safety's sake, disguised as a boy—and set matters straight with her husband.

Pursuing Imogen into the countryside is Cymbeline's stepson, Cloten, who intends to forcibly return her to the fold. Along the way, however, he tangles with banished lord Belarius and his two sons, and is forthwith beheaded for his trouble.

Meanwhile, the war between Rome and Britain has escalated. Posthumus returns to Britain just in time to assist Belarius and his boys (who are actually Cymbeline's sons, kidnapped by Belarius when they were babies) in rallying the British forces. Before all is said and done, the Roman invaders are routed, Posthumus and Imogen are reunited, and there is peace once more in the British Isles.

IMOGEN, daughter to Cymbeline, wife to Posthumus
QUEEN, wife to Cymbeline

CYMBELINE, King of Britain
CLOTEN, stepson to Cymbeline
POSTHUMUS, husband to Imogen
BELARIUS, a banished lord
IACHIMO, an Italian rogue
PISANIO, servant to Posthumus

(1)   IMOGEN   [III.ii.48]

SCENE: A room in Cymbeline's palace

{Imogen has at last received word from her banished husband. In a letter delivered by his manservant, Pisanio, Posthumus informs Imogen that he is hiding out in the Welsh countryside and longs to meet with her there. Unaware that she's being lured into a trap, Imogen is overcome with joyful anticipation.}

O, for a horse with wings! Hear'st thou, Pisanio?   1
He is at Milford-Haven. Read, and tell me
How far 'tis thither. If one of mean affairs
May plod it in a week, why may not I
Glide thither in a day? Then, true Pisanio,   5
Who long'st like me to see thy lord, who long'st—
O, let me bate—but not like me, yet long'st,
But in a fainter kind—O, not like me,
For mine's beyond beyond; say, and speak thick—
Love's counselor should fill the bores of hearing,   10
To th' smothering of the sense—how far it is
To this same blessed Milford. And by th' way
Tell me how Wales was made so happy as
T' inherit such a haven. But first of all,
How we may steal from hence, and for the gap   15
That we shall make in time for our hence-going
And our return, to excuse. But first, how get hence?
Why should excuse be born or ere begot?
We'll talk of that hereafter. Prithee speak,
How many score of miles may we well rid   20
'Twixt hour and hour? I've heard of riding wagers,
Where horses have been nimbler than the sands
That run i' th' clock's behalf. But this is fool'ry.
Go bid my woman feign a sickness, say
She'll home to her father; and provide me presently   25
A riding-suit, no costlier than would fit
A franklin's huswife. Away, I prithee!
Do as I bid thee. There's no more to say.
Accessible is none but the Milford way.

3 mean affairs unimportant, ordinary business   **7 bate** reduce (my estimation of your longing)   **9 thick** quickly   **10 bores of hearing** ears   **11 sense** (of hearing)   **12 by** along   **18 or ere begot** before the need for it arises   **20 rid** ride   **21 'Twixt...hour** between one hour and the next   **riding** racing   **23 i'...behalf** in the place of a clock, i.e., in an hourglass

fool'ry foolishness   **27 franklin's huswife** farmer's housewife   **prithee**
pray thee, beg of you   **29 Accessible is none** there is no other way to go

(2)   IMOGEN   [III.iv.1]

SCENE: The Welsh countryside near Milford-Haven

*{As they near their destination of Milford-Haven (see preceding entry), Pisanio
is about to give Imogen a letter he received from Posthumus. In it is revealed
the true and deadly purpose of their journey.}*

1	Thou told'st me, when we came from horse, the place
	Was near at hand. Ne'er long'd my mother so
	To see me first, as I have now. Pisanio, man,
	Where is Posthumus? What is in thy mind,
5	That makes thee stare thus? Wherefore breaks that sigh
	From th' inward of thee? One but painted thus
	Would be interpreted a thing perplex'd
	Beyond self-explication. Put thyself
	Into a havior of less fear, ere wildness
10	Vanquish my staider senses. What's the matter?
	[*Pisanio offers her a letter.*]
	Why tender'st thou that paper to me, with
	A look untender? If 't be summer news,
	Smile to 't before; if winterly, thou need'st
15	But keep that count'nance still. My husband's hand?
	That drug-damn'd Italy hath outcrafted him,
	And he's at some hard point. [*Reads the letter.*]

"Thy mistress, Pisanio, hath play'd the strumpet in my bed; the testimonies
whereof lies bleeding in me. I speak not out of weak surmises, but from proof
as strong as my grief and as certain as I expect my revenge. That part thou,
Pisanio, must act for me, if thy faith be not tainted with the breach of hers. Let
thine own hands take away her life. I shall give thee opportunity at Milford—
Haven—she hath my letter for the purpose—where, if thou fear to strike and
to make me certain it is done, thou art the pander to her dishonor and equally
to me disloyal."

	False to his bed? What is it to be false?
	To lie in watch there and to think on him?
	To weep 'twixt clock and clock? If sleep charge nature,
	To break it with a fearful dream of him
30	And cry myself awake? That's false to 's bed, is it?
	I false? Thy conscience witness! Iachimo,

Thou didst accuse him of incontinency.
Thou then look'dst like a villain; now methinks
Thy favor's good enough. Some jay of Italy,
Whose mother was her painting, hath betray'd him.   35
Poor I am stale, a garment out of fashion,
And, for I am richer than to hang by th' walls,
I must be ripp'd. To pieces with me! O,
Men's vows are women's traitors! All good seeming,
By thy revolt, O husband, shall be thought   40
Put on for villainy; not born where 't grows,
But worn a bait for ladies.

I came from horse dismounted   **3 first** at birth   **have** (the desire to see
Posthumus)   **6 th' inward** inside   **9 havior** bearing, manner   **of less fear**
less frightening   **wildness** madness   **10 staider** calmer   **13 untender** cold,
unkind   **summer** pleasant   **14 winterly** cheerless, cold   **15 still** i.e., as it is
16 drug-damned damnable for its use of drugs and poisons   **outcraftied**
outwitted, got the best of   **17 hard point** point of crisis   **20 That part**
i.e., of the avenger   **28 'twixt...clock** hour after hour   **sleep charge
nature** sleep should overpower wakefulness   **29 fearful** frightening
31–32 Iachimo...incontinency (In his attempt to corrupt Imogen,
Iachimo falsely claimed that Posthumus was back in Italy indulging himself in
all manner of wanton behaviors; see I.vi.93–148.)   **34 jay** loose woman
35 Whose...painting whose source of beauty is her use of cosmetics
37 for...than because I am too fine   **38 ripp'd** ripped apart, destroyed
39 good seeming that which appears good (in you)   **40 revolt** infidelity
41 not...grows not natural, i.e., genuine, but merely assumed

(3)   IMOGEN   [III.vi.1]

SCENE: Before the cave of Belarius

*{Alone in the Welsh wilderness and still some distance from her destination,
Imogen is compelled by hunger to undertake a chancy exploration.}*

I see a man's life is a tedious one.   1
I have tir'd myself, and for two nights together
Have made the ground my bed. I should be sick,
But that my resolution helps me. Milford,
When from the mountain top Pisanio show'd thee,   5
Thou wast within a ken. O Jove, I think
Foundations fly the wretched—such, I mean,
Where they should be reliev'd. Two beggars told me

I could not miss my way. Will poor folks lie,
10   That have afflictions on them, knowing 'tis
A punishment or trial? Yes; no wonder,
When rich ones scarce tell true. To lapse in fullness
Is sorer than to lie for need, and falsehood
Is worse in kings than beggars. My dear lord,
15   Thou art one o' th' false ones. Now I think on thee,
My hunger's gone; but even before I was
At point to sink for food. [Sees cave.] But what is this?
Here is a path to 't; 'tis some savage hold.
I were best not to call; I dare not call. Yet famine,
20   Ere clean it o'erthrow nature, makes it valiant.
Plenty and peace breeds cowards; hardness ever
Of hardiness is mother. Ho! Who's here?
If any thing that's civil, speak; if savage,
Take or lend. Ho! No answer? Then I'll enter.
25   Best draw my sword; an if mine enemy
But fear the sword like me, he'll scarcely look on 't.
Such a foe, good heavens!

3 should would   **5 show'd** pointed out   **6 within a ken** within sight
7 Foundations . . . wretched charitable institutions seem never to be
available when they are most needed   **8 reliev'd** aided   **10 'tis** i.e., the
afflictions they face, their dire situation   **11 trial** test of virtue   **12 lapse in
fullness** sin while in a state of prosperity   **13 sorer** worse   **14 dear lord**
(referring to Posthumus, albeit ironically, believing as she does that
Posthumus has betrayed her; see preceding entry)   **16 but even** just a
moment   **17 sink for** succumb for lack of   **18 savage hold** animal's
stronghold   **20 Ere . . . nature** before it's able to vanquish life altogether
21 hardness hardship   **23 civil** civilized, well-behaved   **24 Take or lend**
take my life or give me food   **25 an if** if   **27 Such** (grant me) such

(4)   IMOGEN   [IV.ii.291]

SCENE: Before the cave of Belarius

*{Imogen awakens from a much-needed nap only to find next to her a beheaded
corpse adorned in the clothes of her beloved Posthumus. Unaware that the body
is Cloten's and not her husband's, Imogen is understandably devastated.}*

1   Yes, sir, to Milford-Haven; which is the way?
I thank you. By yond bush? Pray, how far thither?

'Od's pittikins! Can it be six mile yet?
I have gone all night. Faith, I'll lie down and sleep.
[*Sees Cloten's body.*]
But soft—no bedfellow? O gods and goddesses!   5
These flow'rs are like the pleasures of the world;
This bloody man, the care on 't. I hope I dream;
For so I thought I was a cave-keeper,
And cook to honest creatures. But 'tis not so;   10
'Twas but a bolt of nothing, shot at nothing,
Which the brain makes of fumes. Our very eyes
Are sometimes like our judgments, blind. Good faith,
I tremble still with fear; but if there be
Yet left in heaven as small a drop of pity   15
As a wren's eye, fear'd gods, a part of it!
The dream's here still. Even when I wake, it is
Without me, as within me; not imagin'd, felt.
A headless man? The garments of Posthumus?
I know the shape of 's leg; this is his hand,   20
His foot Mercurial, his Martial thigh,
The brawns of Hercules; but his Jovial face—
Murder in heaven? How? 'Tis gone. Pisanio,
All curses madded Hecuba gave the Greeks,
And mine to boot, be darted on thee! Thou,   25
Conspir'd with that irregulous devil, Cloten,
Hath here cut off my lord. To write and read
Be henceforth treacherous! Damn'd Pisanio
Hath with his forged letters—damn'd Pisanio!—
From this most bravest vessel of the world   30
Struck the main-top! O Posthumus! Alas,
Where is thy head? Where's that? Ay me, where's that?
Pisanio might have kill'd thee at the heart,
And left this head on. How should this be, Pisanio?
'Tis he and Cloten. Malice and lucre in them   35
Have laid this woe here. O, 'tis pregnant, pregnant!
The drug he gave me, which he said was precious
And cordial to me, have I not found it
Murd'rous to th' senses? That confirms it home.
This is Pisanio's deed, and Cloten. O!   40
Give color to my pale cheek with thy blood,
That we the horrider may seem to those
Which chance to find us. O, my lord, my lord!

1 Yes, sir (No one else is present; Imogen is still half in her dream world.)
2 yond bush that bush over there   **3 'Od's pittikins** God's pity (a common
interjection of the day)   **6 soft** wait   **7 flow'rs** (Belarius spread flowers

about just prior to leaving the cave; see IV.ii.284.)   **8 care on 't** grief of it
9 cave-keeper cave dweller   **10 cook... creatures** (referring to Belarius
and his sons; see III.vi.45–68)   **11 bolt** arrow   **12 fumes** (Dreams were
once believed to be formed by the brain out of bodily vapors.)   **16 As...
eye** as i.e., as the tiny tear shed from a wren's eye   **a** (grant me) a
18 Without outside of   **21 Mercurial** agile, swift (as the foot of Mercury)
Martial powerful (as the leg of Mars)   **22 brawns** muscles   **Jovial** majestic
(as the presence of Jove)   **23 Murder in heaven** i.e., in that this godlike
man has been slain   **24 madded** maddened   **Hecuba** Queen of Troy at the
time of its fall to Greece   **25 darted** thrown   **26 Conspir'd** conspiring
irregulous lawless   **31 Struck the main-top** severed the top of the main
mast (i.e., lopped off his head)   **35 lucre** greed   **36 pregnant** obvious
37 drug (see III.iv.187–91)   **38 cordial** restorative, comforting   **39 home**
utterly, plainly   **40 Cloten** i.e., Cloten's

ALTERNATE
Queen   [I.v.46–82]

HAMLET

Only two months after the untimely death of his father, Hamlet's mother Gertrude has already remarried—and to her late husband's brother, at that. Though Hamlet soon discovers that it was this selfsame uncle of his, Claudius, who murdered King Hamlet in the first place, vengeance is inexplicably slow in coming.

Even as he feigns madness and abuses poor Ophelia, Hamlet continuously agonizes over how best to proceed in the matter before him. When Claudius tumbles to the fact that Hamlet is on to him, he devises an elaborate plot designed to do away with his rival. The plan involves goading Hamlet into a friendly little fencing match with Ophelia's brother, Laertes, during which the Prince is slated to be mortally wounded by a poison-tipped rapier.

All does not go quite as planned, however. Before the final thrusts and parries are made, Hamlet has indeed met his demise... but so too have Gertrude, Laertes, and even Claudius himself.

GERTRUDE, Queen of Denmark, mother to Hamlet
OPHELIA, daughter to Polonius

CLAUDIUS, King of Denmark
HAMLET, son to the late King Hamlet, nephew to Claudius
POLONIUS, counselor to Claudius
HORATIO, friend to Hamlet
LAERTES, son to Polonius
REYNALDO, servant to Polonius
FORTINBRAS, Prince of Norway

(1)   **OPHELIA**   [IV.v.21]

SCENE: A chamber in Elsinore Castle

*{It would seem that the recent demise of her father has pushed Ophelia well over
the edge. Witness this bizarre display of hers before a perplexed Gertrude and
Claudius.}*

1   Where is the beauteous majesty of Denmark?
     [*She begins to sing.*]

          "How should I your true love know
            From another one?
5   By his cockle hat and staff,
            And his sandal shoon.

          He is dead and gone, lady,
            He is dead and gone;
          At his head a grass-green turf,
10   At his heels a stone.

          White his shroud as the mountain snow
            Larded all with flowers;
          Which bewept to the ground did not go
            With true-love showers."

15   They say the owl was a baker's daughter. Lord, we know what we are, but
     know not what we may be. God be at your table! Pray let's have no words of
     this; but when they ask you what it means, say you this:
     [*Sings.*]

          "Tomorrow is Saint Valentine's day,
20   All in the morning betime,
          And I a maid at your window,
            To be your Valentine.
          Then up he rose, and donn'd his clo'es,
            And dupp'd the chamber-door,
25   Let in the maid, that out a maid,
            Never departed more."

     Indeed, la, without an oath, I'll make an end on 't:
     [*Sings.*]

          "By Gis and by Saint Charity,
30   Alack, and fie for shame!
          Young men will do 't, if they come to 't;
            By Cock, they are to blame.

Quoth she, 'Before you tumbled me,
    You promised me to wed.'"
He answers: 35
    "'So would I ha' done, by yonder sun,
    An thou hadst not come to my bed.'"
I hope all will be well. We must be patient, but I cannot choose but weep, to
think they would lay him i' th' cold ground. My brother shall know of it; and so
I thank you for your good counsel. Come, my coach! Good night, ladies; good   40
night, sweet ladies; good night, good night.

5 cockle hat hat with a cockleshell stuck in it   **6 shoon** shoes   **12 Larded**
adorned   **13 bewept** wet with tears **not** (The presence of "not" in this line
makes it run contrary to the sense and meter of the song. Perhaps Ophelia
makes this alteration in order to bring the song into accord with the facts of
her father's burial.)   **15 owl** (alludes to the legend in which a baker's
daughter was turned into an owl for refusing to give Jesus some bread)
19 Saint Valentine's day (This song deals with the popular belief that the
first girl a young man sees on Valentine's day will become his true love.)
24 dupp'd opened up   **29 Gis** Jesus   **30 fie** (an expression of disgust)
32 Cock (a corruption of "God" found in certain oaths of the day)
33 tumbled rolled about with (i.e., had sexual relations with)   **37 An** if
39 him i.e., Polonius

ALTERNATES
Ophelia   [II.i.72–97]
Gertrude   [IV.vii.163–184]

HENRY IV, PART 1

Though Hotspur recently spearheaded England's suppression of a Scottish uprising, he now finds himself consorting with the enemy. Enraged over King Henry's treatment of him concerning the status of some war prisoners, Hotspur joined forces with a few other disenchanted noblemen and mounted his own rebellion.

But when push comes to shove at the Battle of Shrewsbury, most of the conspiracy's forces—namely, those of Mortimer, Glendower, and Hotspur's own father, Northumberland—are conspicuously absent. Outmanned if not outfought, Hotspur is eventually slain by King Henry's son, Prince Hal, and his forces are defeated.

Spicing up the above martial adventures are a series of comedic sideshows featuring the high jinks of the fallen knight Falstaff, King Henry's son, Prince Hal, and others.

LADY PERCY, wife to Hotspur

KING HENRY IV
PRINCE HENRY, also called Prince Hal, son to King Henry IV
EARL OF NORTHUMBERLAND, an English noble
HOTSPUR, son to the Earl of Northumberland
EARL OF DOUGLAS, a Scottish noble, in league with Hotspur
SIR JOHN FALSTAFF, a roguish knight, companion to Prince Henry
EDWARD POINS, friend to Prince Henry

(1)   **LADY PERCY**   [II.III.37]

SCENE: The Earl of Northumberland's castle

{Just as Hotspur has completed his tirade regarding a letter he's just received, Lady Percy enters and makes a game attempt to uncover what it is that's troubling her husband so.}

O, my good lord, why are thus alone?   1
For what offense have I this fortnight been
A banish'd woman from my Harry's bed?
Tell me, sweet lord, what is 't that takes from thee
Thy stomach, pleasure, and thy golden sleep?   5
Why dost thou bend thine eyes upon the earth,
And start so often when thou sit'st alone?
Why hast thou lost the fresh blood in thy cheeks,
And given my treasures and my rights of thee
To thick-ey'd musing and curs'd melancholy?   10
In thy faint slumbers I by thee have watch'd,
And heard thee murmur tales of iron wars,
Speak terms of manage to thy bounding steed,
Cry, "Courage! To the field!" And thou hast talk'd
Of sallies and retires, of trenches, tents,   15
Of palisadoes, frontiers, parapets,
Of basilisks, of cannon, culverin,
Of prisoners' ransom, and of soldiers slain,
And all the currents of a heady fight.
Thy spirit within thee hath been so at war,   20
And thus hath so bestirr'd thee in thy sleep,
That beads of sweat have stood upon thy brow
Like bubbles in a late-disturbed stream,
And in thy face strange motions have appear'd,
Such as we see when men restrain their breath   25
On some great sudden hest. O, what portents are these?
Some heavy business hath my lord in hand,
And I must know it, else he loves me not.

5 stomach appetite   **6 bend** level, direct   **9 my treasures...thee** what I, as your wife, treasure and have certain rights to in you   **10 thick-ey'd** dark and gloomy   **11 watch'd** kept vigil   **12 iron wars** (1) wars of armor and swords (2) harsh, cruel wars   **13 manage** horsemanship   **15 sallies and retires** attacks and retreats   **16 palisadoes** fences made of stakes, used as a form of defense   **frontiers** lesser defensive positions, constructed outside the main area of fortification   **17 basilisks** large cannons   **culverin** particularly long cannons   **19 currents** twists and turns   **heady** headlong, violent   **23 late-disturbed** recently agitated   **24 motions** impulsive movements   **26 hest** behest, command   **27 heavy** weighty, serious

HENRY IV, PART 2

Once again (see *Henry IV, Part 1*), the specter of rebellion appears poised on England's horizon; this time the insurrection is led by the Archbishop of York. Things quickly fall apart, however, when the Archbishop's cause is deserted at the last moment by the Earl of Northumberland. Rather than proceed as planned, the Archbishop instead negotiates a settlement with Prince John. Pursuant to the conditions of said agreement, the Archbishop disbands his army—immediately after which he is arrested and executed. When Northumberland's forces (now back in the game) are subsequently defeated in Yorkshire, the uprising is deemed officially quashed.

But such glad tidings from the battlefield prove to be of little comfort to King Henry; shortly after England's victory, he succumbs to a fatal illness. Assuming Henry's royal responsibilities is his son Prince Hal, who ascends the throne as Henry V.

As in *Henry IV, Part 1*, the amusing misadventures of Falstaff and friends are shuffled in among the narrative's central events. Come story's end, Falstaff gets naught but the bum's rush from the former Prince Hal, his one-time partner in petty crime; the new and improved King Henry orders that the corpulent knight and his cohorts be carted off to prison.

LADY PERCY, widow of Hotspur, daughter-in-law to the Earl of Northumberland

KING HENRY IV
PRINCE HENRY, also called Prince Hal, son to King Henry IV
PRINCE JOHN, son to Henry IV
EARL OF NORTHUMBERLAND, adversary to King Henry IV
ARCHBISHOP OF YORK, adversary to King Henry IV
SIR JOHN FALSTAFF, a roguish knight, companion to Prince Henry

(1)   **LADY PERCY**   [II.III.9]

SCENE: The Earl of Northumberland's castle

{Northumberland feels he is honor-bound to join the rebellion against King Henry, and is preparing to do just that when his daughter-in-law, Lady Percy, intervenes. Her husband, Hotspur, was slain for his efforts in the uprising, and she is not about to stand by and see the same fate befall Hotspur's father.}

For God's sake, go not to these wars!   1
The time was, father, that you broke your word,
When you were more endear'd to it than now,
When your own Percy, when my heart's dear Harry,
Threw many a northward look to see his father   5
Bring up his powers; but he did long in vain.
Who then persuaded you to stay at home?
There were two honors lost—yours and your son's.
For yours, the God of heaven brighten it!
For his, it stuck upon him as the sun   10
In the grey vault of heaven, and by his light
Did all the chivalry of England move
To do brave acts. He was indeed the glass
Wherein the noble youth did dress themselves.
He had no legs that practic'd not his gait;   15
And speaking thick, which nature made his blemish,
Became the accents of the valiant,
For those that could speak low and tardily
Would turn their own perfection to abuse
To seem like him. So that in speech, in gait,   20
In diet, in affections of delight,
In military rules, humors of blood,
He was the mark and glass, copy and book
That fashion'd others. And him, O wondrous him!
O miracle of men! Him did you leave,   25
Second to none, unseconded by you,
To look upon the hideous god of war
In disadvantage; to abide a field
Where nothing but the sound of Hotspur's name
Did seem defensible. So you left him.   30
Never, O never, do his ghost the wrong
To hold your honor more precise and nice
With others than with him! Let them alone.
The Marshall and the Archbishop are strong.
Had my sweet Harry had but half their numbers,   35

Today might I, hanging on Hotspur's neck,
Have talk'd of Monmouth's grave. O, fly to Scotland,
Till that the nobles and the armed commons
Have of their puissance made a little taste.
40 If they get ground and vantage of the King,
Then join you with them, like a rib of steel,
To make strength stronger; but, for all our loves,
First let them try themselves. So did your son;
He was so suff'red. So came I a widow,
45 And never shall have length of life enough
To rain upon remembrance with mine eyes,
That it may grow and sprout as high as heaven,
For recordation to my noble husband.

2 broke your word (Northumberland's last-minute defection was a critical blow to Hotspur's chances for victory in the battle of Shrewsbury. See Henry IV, 1, IV.i.13–85.) **3 endear'd** bound by obligation **6 powers** armies **9 For** as for **13 glass** looking glass **15 He ... gait** only those men without legs failed to imitate his walk **16 thick** quickly **17 accents** manner of speaking **18 tardily** deliberately **21 affections of delight** choice of pleasurable activities **22 humors of blood** temperament **23 mark** pattern **copy** example, model **26 unseconded** unassisted **28 In disadvantage** at a disadvantage (in numbers), outnumbered **abide a field** fight a battle **30 defensible** capable of mounting a defense **32 nice** scrupulous **34 Marshal, Archbishop** Northumberland's fellow insurgents Lord Mowbray and the Archbishop of York, respectively **37 Monmouth's** i.e., Prince Henry's (It was Henry who slew Lady Percy's husband, Hotspur.) **39 their** i.e., the royal forces' **puissance** strength, power **40 get ... vantage** gain position and a strategic advantage **43 try** test **44 suff'red** permitted (to test his strength) **came** became **48 recordation** memorial, tribute

ALTERNATES

HENRY V

Henry readies England for war after his claims on certain lands possessed by the French are ungraciously dismissed by France's royal heir apparent, the Dauphin. Tarrying just long enough to thwart a budding insurgency among a few of his noblemen, Henry and his armies finally cross the channel and embark upon their campaign in France.

After easily capturing the French town of Harfleur, England's forces meet much stiffer opposition when confronted by France's armies near Agincourt. But despite being greatly outnumbered by the French contingent, Henry's armies emerge victorious, and France is forced to sue for peace. Under the terms of surrender, it is agreed that Henry shall marry the French king's daughter, Katharine, and be acknowledged as heir to France's throne.

PRINCESS KATHARINE, daughter to the King of France
HOSTESS, formerly Mistress Quickly, wife to Pistol

KING HENRY V, formerly Prince Henry
BARDOLPH, a rogue
PISTOL, a rogue
LEWIS, THE DAUPHIN, son to the King of France
SIR JOHN FALSTAFF, a roguish knight, R.I.P.

(1)   HOSTESS   [II.III.9]

SCENE: London, before the Boar's Head Tavern in Eastcheap

{Falstaff is no more. The resilient rogue has succumbed to a fatal fever and a "fracted" heart. After Bardolph declares that he would brave Hell just to stand once more with Sir John, Hostess (nee Mistress Quickly) chimes in with a poignant account of the fat knight's final moments.}

1   Nay, sure, Fallstaff's not in hell. He's in Arthur's bosom, if ever man went to Arthur's bosom. 'A made a finer end, and went away an it had been any christom child. 'A parted ev'n just between twelve and one, ev'n at the turning o' th' tide. For after I saw him fumble with the sheets, and play with flowers,
5   and smile upon his fingers' end, I knew there was but one way; for his nose was as sharp as a pen, and 'a babbl'd of green fields. "How now, Sir John?" quoth I, "what man? Be o' good cheer." So 'a cried out, "God, God, God!" three or four times. Now I, to comfort him, bid him 'a should not think of God; I hop'd there was no need to trouble himself with any such thoughts yet. So 'a bade
10   me lay more clothes on his feet. I put my hand into the bed and felt them, and they were as cold as any stone; then I felt to his knees, and so upward and upward, and all was as cold as any stone.

1 Arthur's bosom (Quickly's malapropism for "Abraham's bosom," i.e., heaven; see Luke 16:22)   **2 'A** he   **an** as if   **3 christom** newly christened (Quickly has likely confused "christened" and "Christian.")   **4 play with flowers** fiddle with the bedclothes (that were adorned with flowery patterns?)   **6 pen** quill (A heightened sense of smell was thought to be a sign of approaching death.)

ALTERNATES

Chorus   [I.Prologue]
Chorus   [II.Prologue]
Chorus   [III.Prologue]
Chorus   [IV.Prologue]
Chorus   [V.Prologue]

HENRY VI, PART 1

Mother England's present situation is not a pretty one: Good King Henry V has recently died, his young son is not yet of sufficient age to assume his royal duties as Henry VI, and England's war with France has reached full speed. To make matters worse, a young Frenchwoman by the name of Joan La Pucelle (also known as Joan of Arc) takes the battlefield by storm, inspiring France's forces to one victory after another.

As if that weren't enough, young Henry's game attempt to smooth over a smoldering feud between the Duke of Somerset and the Duke of York has but a transient effect. A tenuous truce between the two houses soon disintegrates into a barrage of mutual recriminations on the French battlefield. Yet, just when England appears on the brink of defeat, Joan of Arc's spiritual mentors suddenly desert her, and France's troops are routed. La Pucelle is subsequently taken prisoner by the Duke of York and burned at the stake.

Meanwhile, the Earl of Suffolk has taken a prisoner of his own: Margaret, daughter to the King of Naples. Suffolk sees Margaret as his personal spoil of war, and by engineering a marriage between her and King Henry, he intends to control both the next queen and the crown.

MARGARET, daughter to the King of Naples, afterward wife to King Henry VI

JOAN LA PUCELLE, a young Frenchwoman, commonly called Joan of Arc

KING HENRY VI

SOMERSET, an English earl, adversary to York

YORK, an English earl, adversary to Somerset

SUFFOLK, also called William De La Pole, an English earl

LORD TALBOT, an English noble

SIR JOHN FALSTAFF

CHARLES, Dauphin of France

DUKE OF BURGUNDY, a French lord

(1)   JOAN LA PUCELLE   [I.ii.72]

SCENE: Before the French city of Orleans

{Charles is about to gather up his troops and go home, since their attempt to
retake Orleans from the English appears to be a lost cause. Enter Joan La Pucelle.
Brimming over with self-assurance, Joan stands convinced that it is she who
has been anointed by heaven to rid France of its Anglican invaders. Seizing her
one chance to sell Charles on the idea, she boldly argues her case.}

1	Dauphin, I am by birth a shepherd's daughter,
	My wit untrain'd in any kind of art.
	Heaven and our Lady gracious hath it pleas'd
	To shine on my contemptible estate.
5	Lo, whilst I waited on my tender lambs,
	And to the sun's parching heat display'd my cheeks,
	God's mother deigned to appear to me
	And in a vision full of majesty
	Will'd me to leave my base vocation
10	And free my country from calamity.
	Her aid she promis'd and assur'd success.
	In complete glory she reveal'd herself;
	And whereas I was black and swart before,
	With those clear rays which she infus'd on me
15	That beauty am I bless'd with which you may see.
	Ask me what question thou canst possible,
	And I will answer unpremeditated.
	My courage try by combat, if thou dar'st,
	And thou shalt find that I exceed my sex.
20	Resolve on this: thou shalt be fortunate
	If thou receive me for thy warlike mate;
	And while I live, I'll ne'er fly from a man.

2 wit mind **art** learning, advanced study   **3 our Lady gracious** the Virgin
Mary   **5 waited on** tended   **13 black and swart** of dark complexion,
swarthy   **14 infus'd** poured   **18 try** put to the test   **20 Resolve on** rest
assured of

(2)   **JOAN LA PUCELLE**   [III.III.41]

SCENE: The plains near Rouen

{Joan attempts to persuade her fellow countryman the Duke of Burgundy to abandon his position with the English forces and renew his allegiance to France.}

Brave Burgundy, undoubted hope of France!   1
Stay, let thy humble handmaid speak to thee.
Look on thy country, look on fertile France,
And see the cities and the towns defac'd
By wasting ruin of the cruel foe.   5
As looks the mother on her lowly babe
When death doth close his tender-dying eyes,
See, see the pining malady of France!
Behold the wounds, the most unnatural wounds,
Which thou thyself hast given her woeful breast.   10
O, turn thy edged sword another way;
Strike those that hurt, and hurt not those that help.
One drop of blood drawn from thy country's bosom
Should grieve thee more than streams of foreign gore.
Return thee therefore with a flood of tears,   15
And wash away thy country's stained spots.
Besides, all French and France exclaims on thee,
Doubting thy birth and lawful progeny.
Who join'st thou with but with a lordly nation
That will not trust thee but for profit's sake?   20
When Talbot hath set footing once in France
And fashion'd thee that instrument of ill,
Who then but English Henry will be lord,
And thou be thrust out like a fugitive?
Call we to mind, and mark but this for proof: 25
Was not the Duke of Orleans thy foe?
And was he not in England prisoner?
But when they heard he was thine enemy,
They set him free without his ransom paid,
In spite of Burgundy and all his friends.   30
See then, thou fight'st against thy countrymen
And join'st with them will be thy slaughter-men.
Come, come, return. Return, thou wandering lord!
Charles and the rest will take thee in their arms.

1 undoubted dauntless, self-assured   **7 tender-dying** dying at a tender age
16 country's stained stained country's   **spots** disgraces, disfigurements
17 exclaims on loudly denounces   **18 progeny** ancestry   **20 but...sake**

except when it profits them to do so   **21 When . . . France** once Talbot has a firm position in France   **22 that** an   **29 ransom paid** (It was common practice to release important prisoners in exchange for the payment of a ransom.)   **30 In spite of** in order to spite   **32 will** who will

(3)   JOAN LA PUCELLE   [V.III.1]

SCENE: The fields near Angiers

{Sensing that the battle—and her powers—are slipping away, Joan calls upon her supernatural benefactors for assistance.}

1	The Regent conquers, and the Frenchmen fly.
	Now help, ye charming spells and periapts,
	And ye choice spirits that admonish me
	And give me signs of future accidents.
5	You speedy helpers, that are substitutes
	Under the lordly monarch of the North,
	Appear and aid me in this enterprise.
	[*Enter fiends.*]
	This speedy and quick appearance argues proof
10	Of your accustom'd diligence to me.
	Now, ye familiar spirits, that are cull'd
	Out of the powerful regions under earth,
	Help me this once, that France may get the field.
	[*They walk, and speak not.*]
15	O, hold me not with silence over-long!
	Where I was wont to feed you with my blood,
	I'll lop a member off and give it you
	In earnest of a further benefit,
	So you do condescend to help me now.
20	[*They hang their heads.*]
	No hope to have redress? My body shall
	Pay recompense, if you will grant my suit.
	[*They shake their heads.*]
	Cannot my body nor blood-sacrifice
25	Entreat you to your wonted furtherance?
	Then take my soul—my body, soul, and all,
	Before that England give the French the foil.
	[*They depart.*]
	See, they forsake me! Now the time is come
30	That France must vail her lofty-plumed crest

And let her head fall into England's lap.
My ancient incantations are too weak,
And hell too strong for me to buckle with.
Now, France, thy glory droopeth to the dust.

1 The Regent i.e., Richard, Duke of York, who was recently named Regent of France   **2 periapts** amulets, charms   **3 choice** excellent   **admonish** warn   **4 accidents** events   **5 substitutes** agents   **6 monarch...North** the devil (Evil spirits were commonly thought to inhabit the northern regions.)   **13 get the field** win on the field of battle   **16 wont** formerly accustomed   **17 I'll now** I'll   **18 earnest** partial payment   **19 condescend** consent, agree   **21 redress** aid   **25 wonted furtherance** usual assistance   **27 foil** defeat   **30 vail** lower   **crest** helmet   **32 ancient** former   **33 buckle with** overcome

(4)   JOAN LA PUCELLE   [V.iv.36]

SCENE: The Duke of York's camp

{Condemned to burn at the stake for being a sorceress, Joan fires off a final salvo at her English captors.}

First, let me tell you whom you have condemn'd: 1
Not me begotten of a shepherd swain,
But issued from the progeny of kings,
Virtuous and holy, chosen from above
By inspiration of celestial grace   5
To work exceeding miracles on earth.
I never had to do with wicked spirits.
But you, that are polluted with your lusts,
Stain'd with the guiltless blood of innocents,
Corrupt and tainted with a thousand vices—   10
Because you want the grace that others have,
You judge it straight a thing impossible
To compass wonders but by help of devils.
No, misconceived! Joan of Arc hath been
A virgin from her tender infancy,   15
Chaste and immaculate in very thought,
Whose maiden blood, thus rigorously effus'd,
Will cry for vengeance at the gates of heaven.
Will nothing turn your unrelenting hearts?
[Then] lead me hence, with whom I leave my curse: 20

May never glorious sun reflex his beams
Upon the country where you make abode,
But darkness and the gloomy shade of death
Environ you, till mischief and despair
25 Drive you to break your necks or hang yourselves!

2 swain peasant **11 want** lack **12 straight** straightaway, immediately
13 compass accomplish **14 misconceived** you who are mistaken
17 rigorously effus'd mercilessly shed **19 turn** change **20 hence** away
from this place **21 reflex** cast **24 Environ** surround

HENRY VI, PART 2

When the Duke of Gloucester dares to criticize certain provisions of England's recent treaty with France—a peace that resulted in, among other things, the marriage of Margaret to King Henry—the new (and seditious) Queen does not take it well. Ably assisted by her fellow conspirators, the Earl of Suffolk and Cardinal Beaufort, Margaret immediately sets about eliminating Gloucester and his influence on the King. Before long Margaret has seen to it that the Duchess of Gloucester is banished, and that Gloucester himself is accused of treason, and ultimately murdered.

Direct from Ireland enters rabble-rouser nonpareil, Jack Cade. Somehow, this oddest of ducks manages to lead a motley crew of insurgents all the way to the streets of London. But the ad hoc rebellion quickly fizzles out when Cade's men accept King Henry's offer of amnesty, and an embittered Jack Cade takes to his heels.

Elsewhere, the Wars of the Roses have begun in earnest. Claiming that he is the rightful King of England, the Duke of York leads his armies to an initial victory over the King's forces at the Battle of St. Alban's, at which point the action moves on to London and *Henry IV, Part 3*.

MARGARET, Queen to King Henry VI
ELEANOR, DUCHESS OF GLOUCESTER, wife to Humphrey

KING HENRY VI
HUMPHREY, DUKE OF GLOUCESTER, uncle to King Henry VI
RICHARD, DUKE OF YORK
LORD SAY, an English noble
JACK CADE, a rebel

(1)   DUCHESS OF GLOUCESTER   [II.iv.19]

SCENE: A street in London

{Found guilty of consorting with witches, the Duchess has been sentenced to life imprisonment on the Isle of Man. While being paraded in disgrace about the streets of London—an ordeal the Duchess must endure as part of her punishment—who should she happen upon but her husband, the Duke of Gloucester.}

1	Come you, my lord, to see my open shame?
	Now thou dost penance too. Look how they gaze!
	See how the giddy multitude do point
	And nod their heads and throw their eyes on thee!
5	Ah, Gloucester, hide thee from their hateful looks,
	And, in thy closet pent up, rue my shame,
	And ban thine enemies, both mine and thine!
	Ah, Gloucester, teach me to forget myself!
	For whilst I think I am thy married wife
10	And thou a prince, Protector of this land,
	Methinks I should not thus be led along,
	Mail'd up in shame, with papers on my back,
	And follow'd with a rabble that rejoice
	To see my tears and hear my deep-fet groans.
15	The ruthless flint doth cut my tender feet,
	And when I start, the envious people laugh
	And bid me be advised how I tread.
	Ah, Humphrey, can I bear this shameful yoke?
	Trowest thou that e'er I'll look upon the world,
20	Or count them happy that enjoy the sun?
	No, dark shall be my light and night my day;
	To think upon my pomp shall be my hell.
	Sometime I'll say, I am Duke Humphrey's wife,
	And he a prince and ruler of the land;
25	Yet so he rul'd and such a prince he was
	As he stood by whilst I, his forlorn duchess,
	Was made a wonder and a pointing-stock
	To every idle rascal follower.
	But be thou mild and blush not at my shame,
30	Nor stir at nothing till the axe of death
	Hang over thee, as sure it shortly will.
	For Suffolk, he that can do all in all
	With her that hateth thee and hates us all,
	And York and impious Beaufort, that false priest,

Have all lim'd bushes to betray thy wings,   35
And fly thou how thou canst, they'll tangle thee.
But fear not thou, until thy foot be snar'd,
Nor never seek prevention of thy foes.

6 closet study, private room **7 ban** curse **10 Protector** (As Lord
Protector of the realm, it was Gloucester's responsibility to oversee the rule
of England until Henry grew beyond childhood.) **12 Mail'd** wrapped (The
Duchess has been shrouded in a white sheet for her public display.)
papers...back a notice which describes the offense for which the Duchess
is being punished has been pinned on her back **14 deep-fet** fetched from
the depths **16 start** wince **envious** malicious, spiteful **17 advised** careful
19 Trowest thou do you suppose **22 pomp** procession in the streets
27 pointing-stock object of ridicule **29 mild** gentle, placid **33 her** i.e.,
Queen Margaret **35 lim'd bushes** put lime on bushes (a common method
of trapping birds) **betray** ensnared **38 seek prevention** try to anticipate
(and thereby thwart) the plots

(2)   QUEEN MARGARET   [III.1.4]

SCENE: The Abbey at Bury St. Edmunds

*{As wife to the impressionable young King Henry, Margaret is a key player in
the conspiracy to dominate England's throne. Here, the Queen does her best to
prejudice Henry against one of the few good and loyal men left in his court, the
Duke of Gloucester.}*

Can you not see? Or will ye not observe   1
The strangeness of his alter'd countenance?
With what a majesty he bears himself,
How insolent of late he is become,
How proud, how peremptory, and unlike himself?   5
We know the time since he was mild and affable,
And if we did but glance a far-off look,
Immediately he was upon his knee,
That all the court admir'd him for submission.
But meet him now, and, be it in the morn,   10
When every one will give the time of day,
He knits his brow and shows an angry eye
And passeth by with stiff unbowed knee,
Disdaining duty that to us belongs.
Small curs are not regarded when they grin,   15

But great men tremble when the lion roars—
And Humphrey is no little man in England.
First note that he is near you in descent,
And, should you fall, he is the next will mount.
20   Me seemeth then it is no policy,
Respecting what a rancorous mind he bears
And his advantage following your decease,
That he should come about your royal person
Or be admitted to your Highness' Council.
25   By flattery hath he won the commons' hearts;
And when he please to make commotion,
'Tis to be fear'd they all will follow him.
Now 'tis the spring, and weeds are shallow-rooted;
Suffer them now, and they'll o'ergrow the garden
30   And choke the herbs for want of husbandry.
The reverent care I bear unto my lord
Made me collect these dangers in the Duke.
If it be fond, call it a woman's fear—
Which fear, if better reasons can supplant,
35   I will subscribe and say I wrong'd the Duke.

2 alter'd adversely changed **5 peremptory** overbearing **6 We** I
(Margaret employs the royal plural) **know** remember **since** when **9 That**
so that **11 give...day** bid good morning **15 grin** bare their teeth, snarl
18 descent lineage **19 mount** ascend to the throne **20 Me seemeth** it
seems to me **policy** prudent conduct of affairs **21 Respecting** considering
22 advantage favorable position **24 Council** a formal body comprising
the king's closest advisors **25 commons'** common peoples' **26 make
commotion** i.e., lead an insurrection **29 Suffer** tolerate **30 husbandry**
proper cultivation **32 collect** perceive, deduce **33 fond** silly
35 subscribe acquiesce, concur

(3)   QUEEN MARGARET   [III.ii.74]

SCENE: A room of state at Bury St. Edmunds

*{When Henry reacts severely to news of Gloucester's death, Margaret counters
with a few histrionics of her own. By distracting her husband, Margaret hopes
to keep him oblivious to the conspiracy that surrounds him.}*

1   What, dost thou turn away and hide thy face?
I am no loathsome leper. Look on me.
What? Art thou, like the adder, waxen deaf?

Be poisonous too, and kill thy forlorn queen.
Is all thy comfort shut in Gloucester's tomb?   5
Why then, Dame Margaret was ne'er thy joy.
Erect his statue and worship it,
And make my image but an alehouse sign.
Was I for this nigh wrack'd upon the sea
And twice by awkward wind from England's bank   10
Drove back again unto my native clime?
What boded this, but well forewarning wind
Did seem to say, "Seek not a scorpion's nest,
Nor set no footing on this unkind shore?"
What did I then but curs'd the gentle gusts   15
And he that loos'd them forth their brazen caves,
And bid them blow towards England's blessed shore,
Or turn our stern upon a dreadful rock?
Yet Aeolus would not be a murderer,
But left that hateful office unto thee.   20
The pretty-vaulting sea refus'd to drown me,
Knowing that thou wouldst have me drown'd on shore
With tears as salt as sea, through thy unkindness.
The splitting rocks cow'r'd in the sinking sands
And would not dash me with their ragged sides,   25
Because thy flinty heart, more hard than they,
Might in thy palace perish Margaret.
As far as I could ken thy chalky cliffs,
When from thy shore the tempest beat us back,
I stood upon the hatches in the storm,   30
And when the dusky sky began to rob
My earnest-gaping sight of thy land's view,
I took a costly jewel from my neck—
A heart it was, bound in with diamonds—
And threw it towards thy land. The sea receiv'd it,   35
And so I wish'd thy body might my heart.
And even with this I lost fair England's view,
And bid mine eyes be packing with my heart,
And call'd them blind and dusky spectacles,
For losing ken of Albion's wished coast.   40
How often have I tempted Suffolk's tongue,
The agent of thy foul inconstancy,
To sit and witch me, as Ascanius did
When he to madding Dido would unfold
His father's acts commenc'd in burning Troy!   45
Am I not witched like her, or thou not false like him?
Ay me, I can no more! Die, Margaret!
For Henry weeps that thou dost live so long.

1 turn away (Distraught over the death of his uncle, Henry has evidently looked away or hidden his face entirely from Margaret and the others.)
3 adder a common viper (Ancient superstition held that adders were deaf.)
waxen grown   **9 nigh** nearly   **wrack'd** shipwrecked (Margaret refers here and afterward to her initial crossing of the English Channel, from the north of France to Dover.)   **10 awkward** unfavorable   **bank** shore   **12 but** but that the   **16 he** i.e., Aeolus, god of the winds   **forth** forth from   **brazen** fortified, impenetrable   **20 office** special duty or charge   **23 salt as** salty as the   **24 splitting rocks** rocks causing ships to split and wreck
26 Because in order that   **27 perish** destroy   **28 ken** see, discern
32 earnest-gaping intensely staring   **38 packing** departed   **heart** (1) literally, her heart-shaped jewel (2) figuratively, her hope   **39 dusky spectacles** dim instruments of vision   **40 Albion's** England's   **wished** desired   **42 agent** (Suffolk was instrumental in arranging Henry and Margaret's marriage.)   **43 witch** bewitch   **Ascanius** (Cupid, disguised as Ascanius, bewitched Queen Dido into falling in love with the real Ascanius's father, Aeneas.)   **44 madding** becoming mad (with love)

ALTERNATE
Queen Margaret   [I.iii.42–82]

HENRY VI, PART 3

When his forces suffer defeat at the first Battle of St. Alban's (see *Henry VI, Part 2*), King Henry has little choice but to strike a bargain with his adversary, the Duke of York. Their agreement calls for Henry to continue ruling England as long as he lives, with York winning official recognition as the royal heir. But since this also amounts to the disinheritance of her son, Queen Margaret declares the arrangement unacceptable.

Joining forces with Lord Clifford, Margaret resolves to wage war against York and his followers. Round one of the ensuing struggle goes to the Queen's faction as York's army is routed at Wakefield, and York himself is stabbed to death by Margaret and Clifford.

York's sons, Edward and Richard, mount an impressive comeback, however. Clifford is slain and the royal forces are defeated at Towton, after which Edward assumes the title of King Edward IV and ascends England's throne.

As for Margaret, her alliance with King Lewis of France proves insufficient to avert a resounding defeat at Tewkesbury. Margaret is taken captive and eventually returned to France in exchange for a healthy ransom. Meanwhile, Margaret's husband suffers a somewhat more dreadful fate: while a prisoner in the Tower of London, Henry is mercilessly butchered by the Duke of Gloucester—a slaying designed to shove Gloucester one step closer to his reign as King Richard III.

QUEEN MARGARET, wife to King Henry VI

KING HENRY VI
LEWIS XI, King of France
LORD CLIFFORD, an English noble in league with Margaret
RICHARD, DUKE OF YORK, adversary to King Henry VI
RICHARD, DUKE OF GLOUCESTER, son to the Duke of York

(1)   QUEEN MARGARET   [I.1.216]

SCENE: The Parliament House

*{King Henry has struck a bargain with the Duke of York. Under terms of the
agreement, Henry will remain monarch of England until he dies, at which time
York shall assume the throne. Soon after learning that her husband has saved
his skin by disinheriting their only son, an irate Margaret confronts Henry with
her impressions of his negotiating savvy.}*

1   Ah, wretched man! Would I had died a maid,
And never seen thee, never borne thee son,
Seeing thou hast prov'd so unnatural a father!
Hath he deserv'd to lose his birthright thus?
5   Hadst thou but lov'd him half so well as I,
Or felt that pain which I did for him once,
Or nourish'd him as I did with my blood,
Thou wouldst have left thy dearest heart-blood there,
Rather than have made that savage Duke thine heir
10   And disinherited thine only son.
Ah, timorous wretch!
Thou hast undone thyself, thy son, and me,
And giv'n unto the house of York such head
As thou shalt reign but by their sufferance.
15   To entail him and his heirs unto the crown,
What is it but to make thy sepulcher
And creep into it far before thy time?
Warwick is chancellor and the lord of Calais;
Stern Falconbridge commands the narrow seas,
20   The Duke is made Protector of the realm,
And yet shalt thou be safe? Such safety finds
The trembling lamb environed with wolves.
Had I been there, which am a silly woman,
The soldiers should have toss'd me on their pikes
25   Before I would have granted to that act.
But thou preferr'st thy life before thine honor;
And seeing thou dost, I here divorce myself
Both from thy table, Henry, and thy bed,
Until that act of parliament be repeal'd
30   Whereby my son is disinherited.
The northern lords that have forsworn thy colors
Will follow mine, if once they see them spread;
And spread they shall be, to thy foul disgrace
And utter ruin of the house of York.

3 unnatural devoid of normal human feelings **6 once** (i.e., during childbirth) **8 there** i.e., in his rightful position as heir to the throne **13 head** free rein **15 entail...unto** appoint he and his offspring as heirs to **19 narrow seas** i.e., the English Channel **20 Duke** the Duke of York **Protector** (As Lord Protector of the realm, it was York's responsibility to oversee the rule of England until Henry grew beyond childhood.) **22 environed with** surrounded by **23 silly** defenseless, feeble **24 pikes** long spear-like weapons **25 granted** agreed, submitted

(2) QUEEN MARGARET [I.iv.66]

SCENE: A field of battle in the English countryside

{The Duke of York has been taken prisoner; his fate now rests upon the mercy of the Queen. But as this monstrous display of hers clearly demonstrates, mercy is not one of Margaret's strong suits.}

Brave warriors, Clifford and Northumberland,	1
Come, make him stand upon this molehill here	
That raught at mountains with outstretched arms,	
Yet parted but the shadow with his hand.	
What, was it you that would be England's king?	5
Was 't you that revel'd in our parliament,	
And made a preachment of your high descent?	
Where are your mess of sons to back you now;	
The wanton Edward, and the lusty George?	
And where's that valiant crook-back prodigy,	10
Dicky your boy, that with his grumbling voice	
Was wont to cheer his dad in mutinies?	
Or, with the rest, where is your darling Rutland?	
Look, York! I stain'd this napkin with the blood	
That valiant Clifford, with his rapier's point,	15
Made issue from the bosom of the boy;	
And if thine eyes can water for his death,	
I give thee this to dry thy cheeks withal.	
[*Gives him the bloodstained cloth.*]	
Alas, poor York, but that I hate thee deadly,	20
I should lament thy miserable state.	
I prithee, grieve, to make me merry, York.	
What, hath thy fiery heart so parch'd thine entrails	
That not a tear can fall for Rutland's death?	
Why art thou patient, man? Thou shouldst be mad;	25

And I, to make thee mad, do mock thee thus.
Stamp, rave, and fret, that I may sing and dance.
Thou would'st be fee'd, I see, to make me sport.
York cannot speak, unless he wear a crown.
30   A crown for York! And lords, bow low to him;
Hold you his hands, whilst I do set it on.
[*Places a paper crown upon his head.*]
Ay, marry, sir, now looks he like a king!
Ay, this is he that took King Henry's chair,
35   And this is he was his adopted heir.
But how is it that great Plantagenet
Is crown'd so soon, and broke his solemn oath?
As I bethink me, you should not be king
Till our King Henry had shook hands with death.
40   And will you pale your head in Henry's glory,
And rob his temples of the diadem,
Now in his life, against your holy oath?
O, 'tis a fault too too unpardonable!
Off with the crown; and with the crown, his head.
45   And, whilst we breathe, take time to do him dead.

3 raught reached   **6 revel'd** rioted   **7 preachment** longwinded and
tiresome speech   **8 mess** group of four   **10 prodigy** freak, monster
12 wont accustomed   **14 napkin** handkerchief (For the encounter between
Clifford and Rutland, which culminates in the latter's death, see I.iii.)
18 withal with   **22 prithee** pray thee, beg you   **25 patient** calm
28 fee'd paid   **make me sport** provide me with amusement   **33 marry**
indeed   **34 took...chair** (see I.i.49)   **37 broke** has broken   **38 bethink
me** think about it, recall   **40 pale** encircle   **41 diadem** royal crown
42 life lifetime   **45 we** I (Margaret is employing the royal plural)   **breathe**
rest

(3)   QUEEN MARGARET   [V.IV.I]

SCENE: The fields of Gloucestershire

*{Though things are looking pretty bleak for Margaret and her cause, the plucky
queen still manages a game attempt at rallying her noblemen and their flagging
spirits.}*

1   Great lords, wise men ne'er sit and wail their loss,
But cheerly seek how to redress their harms.
What though the mast be now blown overboard,

The cable broke, the holding-anchor lost,
And half our sailors swallow'd in the flood?
Yet lives our pilot still. Is 't meet that he   5
Should leave the helm and, like a fearful lad,
With tearful eyes add water to the sea,
And give more strength to that which hath too much,
Whiles, in his moan, the ship splits on the rock,   10
Which industry and courage might have sav'd?
Ah, what a shame; ah, what a fault were this!
Say Warwick was our anchor; what of that?
And Montague our topmast; what of him?
Our slaught'red friends the tackles; what of these?   15
Why, is not Oxford here another anchor?
And Somerset another goodly mast?
The friends of France our shrouds and tacklings?
And, though unskillful, why not Ned and I
For once allow'd the skillful pilot's charge?   20
We will not from the helm to sit and weep,
But keep our course, though the rough wind say no,
From shelves and rocks that threaten us with wrack.
As good to chide the waves as speak them fair.
And what is Edward but a ruthless sea?   25
What Clarence but a quicksand of deceit?
And Richard but a ragged fatal rock?
All these the enemies to our poor bark.
Say you can swim; alas, 'tis but a while.
Tread on the sand; why, there you quickly sink.   30
Bestride the rock; the tide will wash you off,
Or else you famish—that's a threefold death.
This speak I, lords, to let you understand,
If case some one of you would fly from us,
That there's no hop'd-for mercy with the brothers   35
More than with ruthless waves, with sands and rocks.
Why, courage then! What cannot be avoided
'Twere childish weakness to lament or fear.

3 What though what does it matter if **6 meet** proper **9 strength** bulk,
mass (in this case, water) **10 moan** grief **15 tackles** lines used to man a
ship's sails **17 goodly** fine **18 shrouds** sails **19 Ned** her son, Prince
Edward **20 charge** command, responsibility **23 shelves** shoals, sandbanks
wrack destruction, ruin **24 As good** it does as much good **27 ragged**
rough **fatal** menacing **28 bark** a small sailing ship **34 If** in

HENRY VIII

Less a cohesive story than a series of historically related episodes, *Henry VIII* deals with—in order of appearance—Cardinal Wolsey's successful attempt to destroy the Duke of Buckingham; the scandal of Henry's divorce from Queen Katharine and his subsequent marriage to young Anne Bullen; the fall from grace of Cardinal Wolsey; Henry's defense of the Archbishop of Canterbury against charges of heresy; and finally, the christening of Mother England's savior-in-waiting, Princess Elizabeth.

QUEEN KATHARINE, wife to King Henry VIII

KING HENRY VIII
CARDINAL WOLSEY, counselor to King Henry VIII
CARDINAL CAMPEIUS, counselor to King Henry VIII
PORTER'S MAN, a servant at the royal palace

---

(1)   **QUEEN KATHARINE**   [II.iv.13]

SCENE: A hall in London

{After twenty years of marriage, Henry has decided to divorce Katharine. As required by Church edicts, a formal hearing has been convened to consider the matter. When summoned before the court, Katharine "rises out of her chair, goes about the court, comes to the King, and kneels at his feet; then speaks."}

1   Sir, I desire you do me right and justice,
     And to bestow your pity on me; for
     I am a most poor woman, and a stranger,
     Born out of your dominions, having here
5   No judge indifferent, nor no more assurance
     Of equal friendship and proceeding. Alas, sir,
     In what have I offended you? What cause
     Hath my behavior given to your displeasure,
     That thus you should proceed to put me off
10   And take your good grace from me? Heaven witness,

I have been to you a true and humble wife,
At all times to your will conformable;
Ever in fear to kindle your dislike,
Yea, subject to your countenance—glad or sorry,
As I saw it inclin'd. When was the hour   15
I ever contradicted your desire,
Or made it not mine too? Of which of your friends
Have I not strove to love, although I knew
He were mine enemy? What friend of mine
That had to him deriv'd your anger did I   20
Continue in my liking? Nay, gave notice
He was from thence discharg'd? Sir, call to mind
That I have been your wife, in this obedience,
Upward of twenty years, and have been blest
With many children by you. If, in the course   25
And process of this time, you can report,
And prove it too, against mine honor aught—
My bond to wedlock, or my love and duty,
Against your sacred person—in God's name,
Turn me away, and let the foul'st contempt   30
Shut door upon me, and so give me up
To the sharp'st kind of justice. Please you, sir,
The King your father was reputed for
A prince most prudent, of an excellent
And unmatch'd wit and judgment. Ferdinand,   35
My father, King of Spain, was reckon'd one
The wisest prince that there had reign'd by many
A year before. It is not to be question'd
That they had gather'd a wise council to them
Of every realm, that did debate this business,   40
Who deem'd our marriage lawful. Wherefore I humbly
Beseech you, sir, to spare me till I may
Be by my friends in Spain advis'd, whose counsel
I will implore. If not, i' th' name of God,
Your pleasure be fulfill'd!   45

3 poor pitiable **5 indifferent** impartial **6 equal** fair **proceeding** legal
process **9 put me off** reject me **12 conformable** submissive
20 deriv'd drawn, evoked **25 children** (Katharine bore five children while
she was Queen of England, only one of whom—a daughter—lived beyond its
infancy.) **26 process** formal proceeding **27 aught** anything **32 sharp'st**
harshest **33 for** to be **35 wit** intelligence **37–38 by ... before** in many
years **40 Of** from **that** which **41 Who** and who

(2)   QUEEN KATHARINE   [III.1.99]

SCENE: The Queen's apartments

{Two of the King's men, Cardinals Wolsey and Campeius, have come calling on the Queen. In trying to persuade Katharine to go quietly in the matter of her divorce from Henry, Wolsey and Campeius suggest that she rely on the King's "protection" rather than insist upon a formal legal proceeding. Understandably, the Queen suspects that her visitors may be a bit biased on this issue, and makes no bones about telling them so.}

1   Is this your Christian counsel? Out upon ye!
      Heaven is above all yet; there sits a judge
      That no king can corrupt. Holy men I thought ye,
      Upon my soul, two reverend cardinal virtues;
5   But cardinal sins and hollow hearts I fear ye.
      Mend 'em, for shame, my lords! Is this your comfort?
      The cordial that ye bring a wretched lady,
      A woman lost among ye, laugh'd at, scorn'd?
      I will not wish ye half my miseries;
10   I have more charity. But say I warn'd ye.
      Take heed, for heaven's sake, take heed; lest at once
      The burden of my sorrows fall upon ye
      And all such false professors! Would you have me—
      If you have any justice, any pity,
15   If ye be anything but churchmen's habits—
      Put my sick cause into his hands that hates me?
      Alas, h'as banish'd me his bed already;
      His love, too long ago. I am old, my lords,
      And all the fellowship I hold now with him
20   Is only my obedience. What can happen
      To me above this wretchedness? All your studies
      Make me a curse like this.
      Have I liv'd thus long—let me speak myself,
      Since virtue finds no friends—a wife, a true one?
25   A woman, I dare say without vainglory,
      Never yet branded with suspicion?
      Have I with all my full affections
      Still met the King? Lov'd him next heav'n? Obey'd him?
      Been, out of fondness, superstitious to him?
30   Almost forgot my prayers to content him?
      And am I thus rewarded? 'Tis not well, lords.
      Bring me a constant woman to her husband,
      One that ne'er dream'd a joy beyond his pleasure;

And to that woman, when she has done most,
Yet will I add an honor, a great patience.   35
My lord, I dare not make myself so guilty
To give up willingly that noble title
Your master wed me to. Nothing but death
Shall ever divorce my dignities.
Would I had never trod this English earth,   40
Or felt the flatteries that grow upon it!
Ye have angels' faces, but heaven knows your hearts.
What will become of me now, wretched lady?
I am the most unhappy woman living—
Shipwrack'd upon a kingdom, where no pity,   45
No friends, no hope, no kindred weep for me;
Almost no grave allow'd me. Like the lily
That once was mistress of the field and flourish'd,
I'll hang my head and perish.

4 cardinal virtues i.e., justice, prudence, temperance, and fortitude, which make up four of the seven virtues that oppose the seven Deadly Sins **5 cardinal sins** i.e., the seven Deadly Sins   **7 cordial** restorative, something that comforts   **11 at once** all at once   **13 false professors** those who insincerely avow friendship and allegiance   **15 habits** robes **16 sick** woeful, wretched   **17 h'as** he has   **his** from his   **18 old** (At forty-three, Katharine was six years older than Henry.)   **21 studies** religious doctrine and practices (Katharine is asserting that even the cardinals, with all their clerical might, could not devise a more cursed fate for her.)   **23 speak** speak for   **28 Still** always   **29 superstitious** foolishly devoted **32 constant woman** woman who is faithful   **34 most** her best **35 honor** virtue   **36 guilty** deserving of condemnation

ALTERNATES

Anne Bullen   [II.iii.1–35]
Queen Katharine   [II.iv.69–121]
Queen Katharine   [IV.ii.129–173]

JULIUS CAESAR

Fearing that Caesar's immense popularity will one day translate into the end of Roman democracy, Cassius and a few other prominent Roman citizens have decided the time has come for action. The budding conspiracy's final piece falls into place when Brutus's devotion to the republic outweighs even his love for Caesar, and he reluctantly agrees to sign on to the plan.

Shortly after entering the Capitol building, Caesar is surrounded by the group of conspirators, and stabbed to death. Though Brutus manages to tranquilize an irate Roman citizenry with his considerable oratory prowess, the pacifying effect proves short-lived. Mark Antony soon arrives on the scene and, with an impassioned elocutionary display of his own, moves the masses so profoundly that Brutus and the other conspirators are forced to flee.

A triumvirate of Antony, Octavius, and Lepidus is formed to lead Rome and its armies in battle against the forces of Brutus and Cassius. After a series of confrontations, the rebel forces are finally defeated on the plains of Philippi. Rather than face being captured, both Cassius and Brutus elect to die by their own swords.

CALPURNIA, wife to Julius Caesar
PORTIA, wife to Brutus

JULIUS CAESAR
MARK ANTONY, advisor to Caesar, afterward a triumvir
CICERO, a Roman senator
CASCA, conspirator against Julius Caesar
BRUTUS, conspirator against Julius Caesar

(1) **PORTIA** [II.1.233]

SCENE: The garden of Brutus's house

{Convinced that something is weighing heavily on her husband's mind, Portia nobly attempts to share his burden.}

Brutus, my lord, you have ungently   1
Stole from my bed. And yesternight, at supper,
You suddenly arose, and walk'd about,
Musing and sighing, with your arms across;
And when I ask'd you what the matter was,   5
You star'd upon me with ungentle looks.
I urg'd you further; then you scratch'd your head,
And too impatiently stamp'd with your foot.
Yet I insisted, yet you answer'd not;
But, with an angry wafture of your hand,   10
Gave sign for me to leave you. So I did,
Fearing to strengthen that impatience
Which seem'd too much enkindled, and withal
Hoping it was but an effect of humor,
Which sometime hath his hour with every man.   15
It will not let you eat, nor talk, nor sleep;
And could it work so much upon your shape
As it hath much prevail'd on your condition,
I should not know you Brutus. Dear my lord,
Make me acquainted with your cause of grief.   20
Is Brutus sick? And is it physical
To walk unbraced and suck up the humors
Of the dank morning? What, is Brutus sick,
And will he steal out of his wholesome bed
To dare the vile contagion of the night,   25
And tempt the rheumy and unpurged air
To add unto his sickness? No, my Brutus,
You have some sick offense within your mind,
Which by the right and virtue of my place [*She kneels.*]
I ought to know of. And, upon my knees,   30
I charm you, by my once-commended beauty,
By all your vows of love, and that great vow
Which did incorporate and make us one,
That you unfold to me, yourself, your half,
Why you are heavy, and what men tonight   35
Have had resort to you; for here have been
Some six or seven who did hide their faces
Even from darkness. [*She rises.*]

Within the bond of marriage, tell me, Brutus,
40   Is it excepted I should know no secrets
That appertain to you? Am I yourself
But, as it were, in sort or limitation,
To keep with you at meals, comfort your bed,
And talk to you sometimes? Dwell I but in the suburbs
45   Of your good pleasure? If it be no more,
Portia is Brutus' harlot, not his wife.
I grant I am a woman, but withal
A woman that Lord Brutus took to wife.
I grant I am a woman, but withal
50   A woman well-reputed, Cato's daughter.
Think you I am no stronger than my sex,
Being so father'd and so husbanded?
Tell me your counsels; I will not disclose 'em.
I have made strong proof of my constancy,
55   Giving myself a voluntary wound
Here, in the thigh. Can I bear that with patience,
And not my husband's secrets?

4 across folded across your chest (considered a sign of melancholy)
10 wafture wave   **13 enkindled** aroused, animated   **withal** besides,
moreover   **14 humor** a bad mood   **17 shape** appearance   **18 condition**
mental disposition, temper   **21 physical** healthful   **22 unbraced** without
proper attire   **humors** moist airs   **26 rheumy** damp, dank   **unpurged** not
yet cleansed (by the sun's warmth)   **28 sick offense** troublesome illness,
uneasiness   **31 charm** entreat   **34 half** i.e., wife   **35 heavy** disconsolate
36 resort access   **40 excepted** stated as a condition (of the marriage
contract)   **42 in . . . limitation** only to a limited degree   **44 suburbs**
outskirts (In Elizabethan London prostitutes plied their trade in the city's
outskirts.)   **49 withal** at the same time   **50 Cato** (Cato was noted for his
integrity, and was Brutus's uncle as well as his father-in-law.)   **51 my sex** a
typical person of my gender   **53 counsels** secrets   **54 constancy**
self-control   **55 voluntary wound** (In *Lives*, Plutarch reports that Portia, in
an attempt to prove her constancy, "gave herself a deep gash in the thigh,"
and afterward suffered "violent pains and a shivering fever.")

(2)   CALPURNIA   [II.ii.13]

SCENE: Caesar's house

*{Something is very wrong with the world this day, and Calpurnia knows it. It's
no surprise, then, when she tries her level best to keep Caesar at home and out
of harm's way.}*

Caesar, I never stood on ceremonies,   1
Yet now they fright me. There is one within,
Besides the things that we have heard and seen,
Recounts most horrid sights seen by the watch.
A lioness hath whelped in the streets,   5
And graves have yawn'd and yielded up their dead;
Fierce fiery warriors fight upon the clouds,
In ranks and squadrons and right form of war,
Which drizzled blood upon the Capitol;
The noise of battle hurtled in the air,   10
Horses did neigh, and dying men did groan,
And ghosts did shriek and squeal about the streets.
O Caesar, these things are beyond all use,
And I do fear them. When beggars die,
There are no comets seen; the heavens themselves   15
Blaze forth the death of princes. My lord,
Do not go forth today! Call it my fear
That keeps you in the house, and not your own.
We'll send Mark Antony to the Senate-house,
And he shall say you are not well today.   20
Let me, upon my knee, prevail in this.

1 stood on made much of, set store by   **ceremonies** omens, portents
4 watch watchman   **5 whelped** birthed   **6 yawn'd** opened wide   **7 fight**
did fight   **8 right form** precise military formation   **10 hurtled** clattered,
crashed   **13 use** common experience

KING JOHN

Full-scale war between their two countries is apparently averted when England's King John and France's King Philip agree to a royal marriage between John's niece and Philip's son. The truce soon falls by the wayside, however. Under threat of excommunication by the Catholic church, Philip reneges on his agreement with John (whom the Church has declared a heretic), and the war is back on.

England's armies emerge victorious on the battlefield near Angiers, where young Arthur—living in France with his mother, Constance, and arguably the rightful heir to the English throne—is taken captive and returned to England.

Viewing Arthur as a threat to his grip on the crown, John intimates to Hubert De Burgh that it would be better if the boy were dead. Though good Hubert proves unable to commit the foul deed, Arthur dies while attempting to escape.

When word spreads of Arthur's death, a number of English noblemen defect to France, which in turn renews its fight with England. The French invasion founders, though, when Philip the Bastard assumes England's helm and the renegade nobles return to the fold.

King John, meanwhile, has retired to Swinstead Abbey. His death there by poison clears the way for the reign of his son, Henry III.

CONSTANCE, mother to Arthur, widow to King John's brother Geffrey
BLANCHE, a Spanish gentlewoman, niece to King John

KING JOHN
ARTHUR, nephew to King John
EARL OF SALISBURY, an English noble
HUBERT DE BURGH, confidant and aide to King John
PHILIP THE BASTARD, illegitimate son to the late Richard I, nephew to King John
PHILIP, King of France
LEWIS, Dauphin of France, son to King Philip
LYMOGES, DUKE OF AUSTRIA, a member of King Philip's court
CARDINAL PANDULPH, the Pope's legate

(1)   CONSTANCE   [III.1.1]

SCENE: The French King's pavilion

{In order to facilitate peace between their two nations, Philip has agreed to a marriage between his son, Lewis, and King John's niece, Lady Blanche. Since such a union would mean the elimination of Constance's son, Arthur, from the royal picture, her reaction to the plan is quick, cutting, and unequivocal.}

Gone to be married? Gone to swear a peace?   1
False blood to false blood join'd! Gone to be friends?
Shall Lewis have Blanche, and Blanche those provinces?
It is not so; thou hast misspoke, misheard.
Be well advis'd, tell o'er thy tale again.   5
It cannot be; thou dost but say 'tis so.
I trust I may not trust thee, for thy word
Is but the vain breath of a common man.
Believe me, I do not believe thee, man;
I have a king's oath to the contrary.   10
Thou shalt be punish'd for thus frighting me,
For I am sick and capable of fears,
Opress'd with wrongs, and therefore full of fears;
A widow, husbandless, subject to fears,
A woman, naturally born to fears;   15
And though thou now confess thou didst but jest,
With my vex'd spirits I cannot take a truce,
But they will quake and tremble all this day.
What dost thou mean by shaking of thy head?
Why dost thou look so sadly upon my son?   20
What means that hand upon that breast of thine?
Why holds thine eye that lamentable rheum,
Like a proud river peering o'er his bounds?
Be these sad signs confirmers of thy words?
O, if thou teach me to believe this sorrow,   25
Teach thou this sorrow how to make me die,
And let belief and life encounter so
As doth the fury of two desperate men
Which in the very meeting fall and die.
Lewis marry Blanche? O boy, then where art thou?   30
France friend with England, what becomes of me?
Fellow, be gone! I cannot brook thy sight.
This news hath made thee a most ugly man.

1 Gone...married (It was agreed that Lewis and Blanche would be married at once at nearby Saint Mary's chapel.) **2 False** treacherous **3 provinces** (i.e., the French territories which triggered the current dispute...and which

now constitute the bulk of Lady Blanche's dowry)   **4 thou** (Constance is
speaking to the Earl of Salisbury, who was the bearer of these bad tidings.)
5 Be well advised i.e., consider carefully what you've said   **8 vain breath**
false words   **11 frighting** frightening   **12 capable of** susceptible to
17 take a truce make peace   **22 lamentable rheum** sad moisture, tears
23 proud swollen   **peering o'er** flowing over   **30 boy** (referring to Arthur,
who is at her side)   **32 brook** tolerate

(2)   CONSTANCE   [III.i.83]

SCENE: The French King's pavilion

*{No sooner does King Philip proclaim this day of peace between France and
England to be a "holy day," than Constance steps forward to inform both Philip
and the Duke of Austria just what they might do with their hallowed truce.}*

1   A wicked day, and not a holy day!
       What hath this day deserv'd? What hath it done,
       That it in golden letters should be set
       Among the high tides in the calendar?
5   Nay, rather turn this day out of the week,
       This day of shame, oppression, perjury.
       Or, if it must stand still, let wives with child
       Pray that their burdens may not fall this day,
       Lest that their hopes prodigiously be cross'd.
10   But on this day let seamen fear no wrack;
       No bargains break that are not this day made.
       This day, all things begun come to ill end;
       Yea, faith itself to hollow falsehood change!
       You have beguil'd me with a counterfeit
15   Resembling majesty, which, being touch'd and tried,
       Proves valueless. You are forsworn, forsworn!
       You came in arms to spill mine enemies' blood,
       But now in arms you strengthen it with yours.
       The grappling vigor and rough frown of war
20   Is cold in amity and painted peace,
       And our oppression hath made up this league.
       Arm, arm, you heavens, against these perjur'd kings!
       A widow cries; be husband to me, heavens!
       Let not the hours of this ungodly day
25   Wear out the day in peace; but, ere sunset,
       Set armed discord 'twixt these perjur'd kings!
       War, war, no peace! Peace is to me a war.
       O Lymoges, O Austria, thou dost shame

That bloody spoil. Thou slave, thou wretch, thou coward,
Thou little valiant, great in villainy;   30
Thou ever strong upon the stronger side;
Thou Fortune's champion that dost never fight
But when her humorous ladyship is by
To teach thee safety! Thou art perjur'd too,
And sooth'st up greatness. What a fool art thou,   35
A ramping fool, to brag and stamp and swear
Upon my party! Thou cold-blooded slave,
Hast thou not spoke like thunder on my side,
Been sworn my soldier, bidding me depend
Upon thy stars, thy fortune, and thy strength,   40
And dost thou now fall over to my foes?
Thou wear a lion's hide! Doff it for shame,
And hang a calf's-skin on those recreant limbs.

4 high tides great festivals   **8 burdens...fall** children won't be born
9 prodigiously be cross'd be dashed by the birth of a child with monstrous
deformities   **10 But** except that (it should occur)   **wrack** shipwreck   **14 You**
(referring to King Philip)   **14–15 counterfeit Resembling majesty**
counterfeit coin bearing the King's image   **15 touch'd** tested (as one in
olden times would test gold with a touchstone)   **17 arms** armor   **18 in
arms** within your arms (as in an embrace)   **yours** i.e., your blood (referring
to the imminent marriage)   **19 rough** menacing   **20 painted** artificial, false
21 our oppression your oppression of us   **22 perjur'd** false, treacherous
29 spoil (refers to the lion-skin that Austria is wearing, which once belonged
to John's late brother, Richard the Lionheart)   **slave** (used here as term of
general contempt)   **32 champion** warrior   **33 humorous** capricious
ladyship i.e., Fortune, Lady Luck   **35 sooth'st up greatness** flatter the
powerful   **36 ramping** unrestrained   **37 party** behalf   **43 calf's-skin** (an
adornment often worn by jesters)   **recreant** faint-hearted, cowardly

(3)   CONSTANCE   [III.iv.46]

SCENE: The French King's pavilion

*{Moments ago Constance learned that her son had been taken prisoner by the
English. Overwhelmed by grief, she proceeded to tear at her hair and beg for
death. When Cardinal Pandulph interrupts her frenzy by noting that she is
behaving like a madwoman, Constance is quick to reply.}*

My name is Constance; I was Geffrey's wife;   1
Young Arthur is my son, and he is lost
I am not mad; I would to heaven I were!

For then, 'tis like I should forget myself.
5 O, if I could, what grief should I forget?
Preach some philosophy to make me mad,
And thou shalt be canoniz'd, Cardinal.
For, being not mad, but sensible of grief,
My reasonable part produces reason
10 How I may be deliver'd of these woes,
And teaches me to kill or hang myself.
If I were mad, I should forget my son,
Or madly think a babe of clouts were he.
I am not mad. Too well, too well I feel
15 The different plague of each calamity.
And, father Cardinal, I have heard you say
That we shall see and know our friends in heaven.
If that be true, I shall see my boy again;
For since the birth of Cain, the first male child,
20 To him that did but yesterday suspire,
There was not such a gracious creature born.
But now will canker-sorrow eat my bud
And chase the native beauty from his cheek,
And he will look as hollow as a ghost,
25 As dim and meager as an ague's fit,
And so he'll die; and, rising so again,
When I shall meet him in the court of heaven,
I shall not know him. Therefore never, never
Must I behold my pretty Arthur more.
30 Grief fills the room up of my absent child,
Lies in his bed, walks up and down with me,
Puts on his pretty looks, repeats his words,
Remembers me of all his gracious parts,
Stuffs out his vacant garments with his form;
35 Then, have I reason to be fond of grief?
Fare you well! Had you such a loss as I,
I could give better comfort than you do.

1 Geffrey brother to King John and Richard I **3 would** wish **4 like** likely
8 sensible of able to feel **9 reasonable part** mind **reason** an account or
explanation of **13 babe of clouts** rag doll **20 suspire** breathe
21 gracious godly **22 canker-sorrow** sorrow that destroys like a canker
worm (which eats a plant's buds and leaves) **23 native** natural **25 ague's
fit** attack of chills and severe fever **33 Remembers** reminds

ALTERNATE
Constance [III.i.43–74]

KING LEAR

Lear's plan to divide his kingdom among his three daughters hits a snag when his youngest child, Cordelia, refuses to join her two older sisters in showering their father with disingenuous praise. Goneril and Regan thus split the spoils in half, while Cordelia rebounds from her disinheritance by marrying the King of France.

The madness of Lear's method soon becomes evident, however, when both Goneril and Regan humiliate the King by refusing to accommodate his retinue of boisterous knights. Enraged by his daughters' ingratitude, Lear storms off into the tempestuous night.

Elsewhere, the Earl of Gloucester has his own problems. Through a series of sinister machinations, the Earl has been convinced by his bastard son Edmund that his other (and legitimate) son, Edgar, covets his wealth and wishes him dead. Edgar, fearing for his life, takes on the guise of a madman and escapes into the countryside. It is there that, sometime later, Edgar encounters his father, who has been blinded by Regan's husband Cornwall for providing assistance to Lear. Both the blind Gloucester, led by his son Edgar, and the mad Lear, aided by his true friend Kent, end up near Dover, where Cordelia has landed with French troops in order to rescue her father. Cordelia is reunited with her father, but her soldiers suffer defeat at the hands of Edmund and his forces, and both Cordelia and Lear are taken captive.

Before all the shouting is over, Cordelia is hanged by order of Edmund, Goneril poisons Regan before dying by her own hand, Edmund is slain by Edgar, and poor old Lear dies of grief.

GONERIL, daughter to Lear
REGAN, daughter to Lear
CORDELIA, daughter to Lear

LEAR, King of Britain
DUKE OF ALBANY, husband to Goneril
EARL OF KENT, an English noble, friend to Lear
EARL OF GLOUCESTER, an English noble
EDGAR, son to Gloucester
EDMUND, illegitimate son to Gloucester
OSWALD, steward to Goneril

(1)   **GONERIL**   [I.IV.200]

SCENE: The Duke of Albany's palace

{To hear Goneril tell it, it's been one wild party after another ever since Lear and his followers came to stay at her place. Having had her fill of riotous behavior, she's about to inform Lear of some new house rules.}

1   Not only, sir, this your all-licens'd fool,
      But other of your insolent retinue
      Do hourly carp and quarrel, breaking forth
      In rank and not-to-be-endured riots. Sir,
5   I had thought, by making this well known unto you,
      To have found a safe redress, but now grow fearful,
      By what yourself too late have spoke and done,
      That you protect this course and put it on
      By your allowance; which if you should, the fault
10   Would not scape censure, nor the redresses sleep,
      Which, in the tender of a wholesome weal,
      Might in their working do you that offense
      Which else were shame, that then necessity
      Will call discreet proceeding.
15   I would you would make use of your good wisdom,
      Whereof I know you are fraught, and put away
      These dispositions which of late transport you
      From what you rightly are. I do beseech you
      To understand my purposes aright.
20   As you are old and reverend, should be wise.
      Here do you keep a hundred knights and squires,
      Men so disorder'd, so debosh'd and bold,
      That this our court, infected with their manners,
      Shows like a riotous inn. Epicurism and lust
25   Makes it more like a tavern or a brothel
      Than a grac'd palace. The shame itself doth speak
      For instant remedy. Be then desir'd
      By her, that else will take the thing she begs,
      A little to disquantity your train,
30   And the remainders that shall still depend
      To be such men as may besort your age,
      Which know themselves and you.

1 all-licens'd permitted to say and do anything he likes   **4 riots**
unrestrained revelry, debauchery   **6 safe** certain   **fearful** alarmed,
apprehensive   **7 too late** all too recently   **8 put it on** encourage it
9 allowance approval   **10 scape** escape   **redresses sleep** punishments

(for this riotous behavior) lie dormant   **11 tender of** deep regard for **wholesome weal** peaceful and prosperous state   **13 else were** under other circumstances would be regarded as **then necessity** the necessity of the times   **14 discreet** wise, prudent   **15 I would** I wish   **16 fraught** amply provided   **17 dispositions** wanton behaviors, eccentric moods **19 aright** correctly   **20 should** you should   **22 debosh'd** debauched **bold** rude   **24 Shows like** has the appearance of   **Epicurism** gluttony, self-indulgence   **26 grac'd** dignified, honorable   **speak** i.e., cry out **29 disquantity your train** reduce the number of your followers   **30 the remainders** those who remain   **depend** be your dependents   **31 besort** befit

ALTERNATE
Regan   [IV.v.9–40]

LOVE'S LABOR'S LOST

No sooner do the King of Navarre and three of his lords forswear the company of women for the next three years than up pops the Princess of France for a diplomatic visit. Naturally, the King proceeds to fall head over heels for the Princess, even as each of his lords is in turn smitten by one of the Princess's ladies. Before long the "No Women" rule is a rule in name only.

Elsewhere, the Spaniard Don Armado has managed to quell his own passion for a country lass named Jaquenetta long enough to prepare an evening's entertainment for the King and his guests. The merry presentation is going just swell until news from France arrives that the Princess's father has died.

Though the Princess is compelled to return home at once, she and her ladies indicate that wedding bells within a year's time is a distinct possibility—if their would-be husbands behave themselves in the interim.

PRINCESS OF FRANCE
ROSALINE, lady attending on the Princess of France
JAQUENETTA, a country girl

FERDINAND, King of Navarre
BEROWNE, lord attending on the King
LONGAVILLE, lord attending on the King
DUMAINE, lord attending on the King
DON ARMADO, an eccentric Spaniard
HOLOFERNES, a schoolmaster

(1)　　　　　　　**PRINCESS OF FRANCE**　　　　　[V.II.777]

SCENE: The King of Navarre's park

{The arrival of sad news—the Princess's father has died—obliges the Princess to return immediately to France. But first, a moment to tie up some loose ends with the King of Navarre and his lords.}

We have receiv'd your letters full of love;　　　　　　　　　1
Your favors, the ambassadors of love;
And, in our maiden council, rated them
At courtship, pleasant jest, and courtesy,
As bombast and as lining to the time.　　　　　　　　　　5
But more devout than this in our respects
Have we not been, and therefore met your loves
In their own fashion, like a merriment.
Now, at the latest minute of the hour,
Is a time, methinks, too short　　　　　　　　　　　　　10
To make a world-without-end bargain in.
No, no, my lord, your Grace is perjur'd much,
Full of dear guiltiness; and therefore this:
If for my love (as there is no such cause)
You will do aught, this shall you do for me:　　　　　　　15
Your oath I will not trust, but go with speed
To some forlorn and naked hermitage,
Remote from all the pleasures of the world;
There stay until the twelve celestial signs
Have brought about the annual reckoning.　　　　　　　20
If this austere insociable life
Change not your offer made in heat of blood;
If frosts and fasts, hard lodging, and thin weeds
Nip not the gaudy blossoms of your love,
But that it bear this trial, and last love;　　　　　　　25
Then, at the expiration of the year,
Come challenge me, challenge me by these deserts,
[*She gives him her hand.*]
And, by this virgin palm now kissing thine,
I will be thine; and till that instant shut　　　　　　　30
My woeful self up in a mourning house,
Raining the tears of lamentation
For the remembrance of my father's death.
If this thou do deny, let our hands part,
Neither intitled in the other's heart.　　　　　　　　　35

2 favors gifts, tokens of affection (see V.ii.1)   **3 rated** evaluated   **4 At** as merely   **5 bombast** loosely wound material used to pad or stuff garments   **6 devout** serious **respects** regard, considerations   **10 methinks** it seems to me   **11 world-without-end** everlasting   **12 perjur'd** forsworn   **13 dear** extreme, grievous   **15 aught** anything   **17 naked** austere   **19 twelve celestial signs** signs of the zodiac   **20 annual reckoning** i.e., passing of one year   **21 insociable** unsociable   **22 blood** passion   **23 hard** harsh **weeds** garments   **24 gaudy** showy   **25 last** continue as   **27 challenge** claim **by these deserts** on the basis of these actions meriting reward   **35 intitled in** having a legal claim on

(2)   ROSALINE   [V.II.841]

SCENE: The King of Navarre's park

{Rosaline remains skeptical of Berowne's vows of love. To test his resolve in the matter, she offers a proposal of her own.}

1   Oft have I heard of you, my Lord Berowne,
       Before I saw you; and the world's large tongue
       Proclaims you for a man replete with mocks,
       Full of comparisons and wounding flouts,
5   Which you on all estates will execute
       That lie within the mercy of your wit.
       To weed this wormwood from your fruitful brain,
       And therewithal to win me, if you please—
       Without the which I am not to be won—
10   You shall this twelvemonth term from day to day
       Visit the speechless sick and still converse
       With groaning wretches; and your task shall be,
       With all the fierce endeavor of your wit
       To enforce the pained impotent to smile.
15   [For] that's the way to choke a gibing spirit,
       Whose influence is begot of that loose grace
       Which shallow laughing hearers give to fools.
       A jest's prosperity lies in the ear
       Of him that hears it, never in the tongue
20   Of him that makes it. Then, if sickly ears,
       Deaf'd with the clamors of their own dear groans,
       Will hear your idle scorns, continue then,
       And I will have you and that fault withal;

But if they will not, throw away that spirit,
And I shall find you empty of that fault,
Right joyful of your reformation.

25

2 the ... tongue the general word, universal report   **3 mocks** sneers,
derisive remarks   **4 comparisons** sarcastic figures of speech   **flouts** insults
5 all estates all classes of people   **7 wormwood** bitterness
8 therewithal at the same time   **11 still converse** continually associate
14 enforce induce   **pained impotent** those rendered helpless by their pain
and suffering   **15 gibing** taunting, derisive   **spirit** disposition, temperament
16 influence inspiration   **16–17 loose ... hearers** easily-won approval,
which those who laugh at anything   **18 prosperity** success   **21 Deaf'd**
with deafened by   **dear** dire   **23 withal** as well

ALTERNATE
Princess of France   [II.i.13–34]

MACBETH

On his way home from a successful military campaign, Macbeth encounters three witches who hail him as Thane of Cawdor and "king hereafter." When word soon arrives that King Duncan has in fact named Macbeth as the new Thane of Cawdor, Macbeth starts to thinking. Before long, his lust for the crown—not to mention Lady Macbeth's prodding—have turned those thoughts to murder. After weathering a few fleeting pangs of conscience, Macbeth slays Duncan in his sleep, and is crowned king.

Though Duncan's sons, Malcolm and Donalbain, are initially suspected of the King's murder, it isn't long before Macbeth emerges as the true culprit. When Macbeth's former comrade, Macduff, convinces Malcolm to fight for his rightful place on the Scottish throne, Macbeth's fate seems all but sealed.

Left twisting in the wind by his friends and Lady Macbeth (who descends into madness and kills herself), Macbeth is eventually set upon by Macduff in the fields of Dunsinane, and is slain. Soon thereafter, Malcolm is hailed as the new King of Scotland.

LADY MACBETH, wife to Macbeth
HECATE, mistress of witches
WITCHES, underlings to Hecate

DUNCAN, King of Scotland
MALCOLM, son to Duncan
DONALBAIN, son to Duncan
MACBETH, a general of the King's army
BANQUO, a general of the King's army
MACDUFF, a Scottish noble and officer of the King's army

(1)   LADY MACBETH   [I.v.1]

SCENE: Macbeth's castle

{Alone within the castle walls, Lady Macbeth reads over a letter that she has
just received from her husband. In it, Macbeth notes his recent success on the
battlefield . . . and mentions something about a bizarre encounter with three
"weird sisters."}

"They met me in the day of success; and I have learn'd by the perfect'st report   1
they have more in them than mortal knowledge. When I burnt in desire to
question them further, they made themselves air, into which they vanish'd.
Whiles I stood rapt in the wonder of it, came missives from the King, who all-
hail'd me 'Thane of Cawdor,' by which title, before, these weird sisters saluted   5
me, and referr'd me to the coming on of time with 'Hail, king that shalt be!'
This have I thought good to deliver thee, my dearest partner of greatness, that
thou mightst not lose the dues of rejoicing by being ignorant of what greatness
is promis'd thee. Lay it to thy heart, and farewell."
Glamis thou art, and Cawdor, and shalt be   10
What thou art promis'd. Yet do I fear thy nature;
It is too full o' th' milk of human kindness
To catch the nearest way. Thou wouldst be great,
Art not without ambition, but without
The illness should attend it. What thou wouldst highly,   15
That wouldst thou holily; wouldst not play false,
And yet wouldst wrongly win. Thou'dst have, great Glamis,
That which cries "Thus thou must do," if thou have it;
And that which rather thou dost fear to do
Than wishest should be undone. Hie thee hither,   20
That I may pour my spirits in thine ear,
And chastise with the valor of my tongue
All that impedes thee from the golden round,
Which fate and metaphysical aid doth seem
To have thee crown'd withal. Come, you spirits   25
That tend on mortal thoughts; unsex me here,
And fill me from the crown to the toe top-full
Of direst cruelty! Make thick my blood;
Stop up th' access and passage to remorse,
That no compunctious visitings of nature   30
Shall my fell purpose, nor keep peace between
Th' effect and it! Come to my woman's breasts,
And take my milk for gall, you murd'ring ministers,
Wherever in your sightless substances
You wait on nature's mischief! Come, thick night,   35

And pall thee in the dunnest smoke of hell,
That my keen knife see not the wound it makes,
Nor heaven peep through the blanket of the dark,
To cry "Hold, hold!"

1 success (i.e., victory over local insurgents and Norwegian invaders; see I.ii.11 and I.ii.33) **perfect'st** most accurate and reliable   **2 mortal knowledge** that which is known to mankind   **4 missives** messengers
5 Thane a Scottish title roughly equivalent to "Earl"   **7 deliver** report to, inform   **10 Glamis, Cawdor** (Macbeth now possesses two titles Thane of Glamis, and the title recently bestowed upon him by Duncan, Thane of Cawdor.)   **11 do I fear** I am apprehensive about   **13 nearest** most opportune   **15 illness should** wickedness that should   **19–20 And... undone** i.e., and your dread of doing what must be done outstrips your desire to see it accomplished   **20 Hie** hasten   **21 spirits** sentiments, convictions   **23 round** crown   **24 metaphysical** supernatural   **25 withal** with   **26 tend on mortal** attend on deadly   **27 crown** head
29 remorse compassion, pity   **30 nature** natural feeling or compassion
31 fell deadly, cruel   **keep peace** intervene   **32 Th' effect and it** my objective and its fulfillment   **33 for** in exchange for   **ministers** agents
34 sightless substances invisible forms   **35 wait on** assist   **36 pall** shroud, wrap   **dunnest** darkest

(2)   Lady Macbeth   [I.vii.35]

SCENE: An inner courtyard of Macbeth's castle

{As the fateful hour approaches, Macbeth is having some serious second thoughts about murdering Duncan. Lady Macbeth, on the other hand, is steady and certain as ever. At once chiding and encouraging her husband, she moves to bolster Macbeth's faltering resolve.}

1   Was the hope drunk
     Wherein you dress'd yourself? Hath it slept since?
     And wakes it now, to look so green and pale
     At what it did so freely? From this time
5   Such I account thy love. Art thou afeard
     To be the same in thine own act and valor
     As thou art in desire? Wouldst thou have that
     Which thou esteem'st the ornament of life,
     And live a coward in thine own esteem,
10   Letting "I dare not" wait upon "I would,"

Like the poor cat i' th' adage? What was 't, then,
That made you break this enterprise to me?
When you durst do it, then you were a man;
And, to be more than what you were, you would
Be so much more the man. Nor time nor place   15
Did then adhere, and yet you would make both.
They have made themselves, and that their fitness now
Does unmake you. I have given suck, and know
How tender 'tis to love the babe that milks me;
I would, while it was smiling in my face,   20
Have pluck'd my nipple from its boneless gums
And dash'd the brains out, had I so sworn as you
Have done to this.
But screw your courage to the sticking-place,
And we'll not fail. When Duncan is asleep—   25
Whereto the rather shall his day's hard journey
Soundly invite him—his two chamberlains
Will I with wine and wassail so convince,
That memory, the warder of the brain,
Shall be a fume, and the receipt of reason   30
A limbeck only. When in swinish sleep
Their drenched natures lie as in a death,
What cannot you and I perform upon
Th' unguarded Duncan? What not put upon
His spongy officers, who shall bear the guilt   35
Of our great quell? Who dares receive it other,
As we shall make our griefs and clamor roar
Upon his death?

3 green sickly **8 ornament of life** i.e., crown **11 adage** (refers to the saying, "the cat would eat fish, and would not wet her feet") **12 break** broach **13 durst** dared to **15 Nor time** neither time **16 Did then adhere** were then suitable **would** wanted to **17 that their fitness** their very suitability **18 unmake** undo, unnerve **given suck** nursed an infant **24 But** only, just **sticking-place** place in which a thing comes to rest and holds fast **26 the rather** the sooner, the more readily **hard journey** (i.e., the ride to Macbeth's castle) **27 chamberlains** servants who attend the king in his bedchamber **28 wassail** spiced ale **convince** overwhelm **29 warder** caretaker, watchman **30 fume** (It was thought that the fumes of consumed wine rose from the stomach to the head, thereby intoxicating the brain and clouding one's reason.) **receipt** receptacle **31 limbeck** the upper part of a distillery, to which the fumes rise **swinish** gross, lacking sensitivity **34 put upon** blame on **35 spongy** saturated (with drink) **36 quell** murder, assassination **receive it other** perceive it otherwise **37 As** inasmuch as

(3)   **HECATE**   [III.v.2]

SCENE: The Scottish countryside

{Hecate meets up with the three weird sisters. Clearly, she's displeased with their meddling in Macbeth's affairs, and she makes no bones about telling them so.}

1	Have I not reason, bedlams as you are,
	Saucy and overbold? How did you dare
	To trade and traffic with Macbeth
	In riddles and affairs of death;
5	And I, the mistress of your charms,
	The close contriver of all harms,
	Was never call'd to bear my part,
	Or show the glory of our art?
	And, which is worse, all you have done
10	Hath been but for a wayward son,
	Spiteful and wrathful, who, as others do,
	Loves for his own ends, not for you.
	But make amends now. Get you gone,
	And at the pit of Acheron
15	Meet me i' th' morning; thither he
	Will come to know his destiny.
	Your vessels and your spells provide,
	Your charms and every thing beside.
	I am for th' air; this night I'll spend
20	Unto a dismal and fatal end.
	Great business must be wrought ere noon.
	Upon the corner of the moon
	There hangs a vap'rous drop profound;
	I'll catch it ere it come to ground.
25	And that, distill'd by magic sleights,
	Shall raise such artificial sprites
	As by the strength of their illusion
	Shall draw him on to his confusion.
	He shall spurn fate, scorn death, and bear
30	His hopes 'bove wisdom, grace, and fear.
	And you all know security
	Is mortals' chiefest enemy. [*Music is heard.*]
	Hark! I am call'd; my little spirit, see,
	Sits in a foggy cloud, and stays for me.

1 reason (Hecate is responding to an observation made by one of the sisters that she looked "angerly.") **bedlams** hags **3 traffic** have dealings with **5 charms** magic spells, enchantments **6 close** secret **14 Acheron**

the river of Hades (here representing Hell itself)   **20 dismal** sinister
23 profound (1) of great significance (2) i.e., ready to drop off   **25 sleights** .
methods   **26 artificial** produced by magic   **27 illusion** deception
28 confusion destruction   **31 security** overconfidence   **34 stays** waits

(4)   LADY MACBETH   [V.1.31]

SCENE: Macbeth's castle

*{It's evident that the murders of Duncan and Banquo are weighing heavily on
Lady Macbeth's conscience. In what is but the latest of the lady's somnambulant
strolls, her troubled psyche struggles to come to terms with her heinous deeds.}*

Yet here's a spot. Out, damned spot! Out, I say! One—two—why then 'tis time   1
to do 't. Hell is murky. Fie, my lord, fie; a soldier, and afeard? What need we
fear who knows it, when none can call our pow'r to account? Yet who would
have thought the old man to have had so much blood in him? The Thane of Fife
had a wife; where is she now?—What, will these hands ne'er be clean?—No   5
more o' that, my lord, no more o' that; you mar all this with starting. Here's
the smell of the blood still. All the perfumes of Arabia will not sweeten this
little hand. Oh, oh, oh! Wash your hands, put on your nightgown; look not so
pale! I tell you yet again, Banquo's buried; he cannot come out on 's grave. To
bed, to bed! There's knocking at the gate. Come, come, come, come, give me   10
your hand. What's done cannot be undone. To bed, to bed, to bed!

2 Fie a term used to express shock or disgust   **3 it** (referring to their
murderous deeds)   **4 old man** (referring to Duncan)   **Thane** a Scottish
title, roughly equivalent to "Earl"   **6 starting** startled movements   **9 on 's**
of his

MEASURE FOR MEASURE

Duke Vincentio has made known his intention to leave Vienna and turn control of the city over to his deputy, Angelo. But in fact, it's all a ruse. After merely pretending to leave town, the Duke adopts the guise of a friar so that he might clandestinely observe local events as they unfold.

Suddenly flush with power, Deputy Angelo immediately sets about addressing what he views as the city's declining morality. First up is the sentencing of young Claudio to death for impregnating his girlfriend, Juliet, before the two could be legally married. When Claudio's sister, Isabella, appears before Angelo to beg that he spare her brother's life, Angelo agrees to do just that—if she agrees to be his mistress. Unable to compromise her honor, Isabella spurns the deputy's vile offer and informs Claudio that she cannot save him.

Just in the nick of time, reenter Duke Vincentio. After orchestrating a bit of intrigue that involved Angelo's former betrothed, Mariana, the Duke dispenses with his friar disguise, spares Claudio's life, condemns Angelo's hypocrisy (even as he compels him to wed Mariana), and to top things off, requests for himself Isabella's hand in marriage.

ISABELLA, sister to Claudio
MARIANA, betrothed to Angelo

VINCENTIO, the Duke of Vienna
ANGELO, deputy to the Duke Vincentio
CLAUDIO, a young gentleman, brother to Isabella

(1)   ISABELLA   [II.ii.27]

SCENE: Angelo's house

{Isabella has temporarily shelved her plans to enter a nunnery in order to come to the aid of her brother, Claudio. Though his transgression was a minor one, the imprisoned Claudio has been sentenced to pay for it with his life. So it is that Isabella now stands before Vienna's deputy, Angelo, to plead for mercy and her brother's life.}

I am a woeful suitor to your honor;   1
Please but your honor hear me.
There is a vice that most I do abhor,
And most desire should meet the blow of justice,
For which I would not plead, but that I must;   5
For which I must not plead, but that I am
At war betwixt will and will not.
I have a brother is condemn'd to die.
I do beseech you, let it be his fault,
And not my brother. Must he needs die?   10
I do think that you might pardon him,
And neither heaven nor man grieve at the mercy.
No ceremony that to great ones 'longs,
Not the king's crown, nor the deputed sword,
The marshal's truncheon, nor the judge's robe,   15
Become them with one half so good a grace
As mercy does.
If he had been as you and you as he,
You would have slipp'd like him; but he, like you,
Would not have been so stern.   20
I would to heaven I had your potency,
And you were Isabel! Should it then be thus?
No. I would tell what 'twere to be a judge,
And what a prisoner. How would you be,
If He, which is the top of judgment, should   25
But judge you as you are? O, think on that,
And mercy then will breathe within your lips,
Like man new made. O, it is excellent
To have a giant's strength, but it is tyrannous
To use 't like a giant. Could great men thunder   30
As Jove himself does, Jove would never be quiet,
For every pelting, petty officer
Would use his heaven for thunder,

Nothing but thunder! Merciful Heaven,
35   Thou rather with thy sharp and sulpherous bolt
Splits the unwedgeable and gnarled oak
Than the soft myrtle; but man, proud man,
Dress'd in a little brief authority,
Most ignorant of what he's most assur'd,
40   His glassy essence, like an angry ape,
Plays such fantastic tricks before high heaven
As makes the angels weep; who, with our spleens,
Would all themselves laugh mortal.
We cannot weigh our brother with ourself.
45   Great men may jest with saints; 'tis wit in them,
But in the less foul profanation.
That in the captain's but a choleric word,
Which in the soldier is flat blasphemy.
Authority, though it err like others,
50   Hath yet a kind of medicine in itself,
That skins the vice o' th' top. Go to your bosom,
Knock there, and ask your heart what it doth know
That's like my brother's fault. If it confess
A natural guiltiness such as is his,
55   Let it not sound a thought upon your tongue
Against my brother's life.

9 let ... fault (i.e., let it be his crime that is to be condemned)
13 ceremony symbol of authority **'longs** belongs **14 deputed sword**
the sword of justice **15 truncheon** staff borne by military officers **19 like
you** in your position (of authority) **21 potency** power, authority **23 tell**
know **25 He** i.e., God **top of judgment** supreme judge **28 Like...
made** as if you were a new and different man **31 be quiet** have any peace
32 pelting paltry **officer** official **35 sulpherous** having the qualities of
burning sulpher **37 proud** arrogant **38 brief** short-lived **39 assured**
assured of (i.e., his "glassy essence") **40 glassy essence** i.e., frail and
mirror-like (in that it reflects his godlike soul) essential being **like...ape**
(The sense here is that when a man attempts to play the role of a god, he is
as pitiful and ridiculous as the ape who tries to imitate a man.) **42 with our
spleens** if they had temperaments like ours (The spleen was thought to be
the seat of emotions.) **43 themselves laugh mortal** laugh as if they were
mortals **44 weigh ... ourself** judge others by the same standards as we
judge ourself **45 jest with** make jokes about **46 the less** lesser men (it is)
51 skins ... top covers the sore with skin (i.e., hides, but does not redress,
transgressions it has committed)

(2)   **MARIANA**   [V.I.184]

SCENE: The city gate

{Mariana stands before the Duke and everyone else to both defend and condemn her former betrothed, Angelo. Sporting a veil to conceal her true identity, she slowly begins to unravel the web of deception woven by her, Isabella, and a wily friar.}

My lord, I do confess I ne'er was married,   I
And I confess besides I am no maid.
I have known my husband, yet my husband
Knows not that ever he knew me.
She that accuses him of fornication,   5
In selfsame manner doth accuse my husband,
And charges him, my lord, with such a time
When I'll depose I had him in mine arms
With all th' effect of love. Now I will unmask.
[*She removes her veil, and confronts Angelo.*]   10
This is that face, thou cruel Angelo,
Which once thou swor'st was worth the looking on;
This is the hand which, with a vow'd contract,
Was fast belock'd in thine; this is the body
That took away the match from Isabel,   15
And did supply thee at thy garden-house
In her imagin'd person. Noble Prince,
As there comes light from heaven and words from breath,
As there is sense in truth and truth in virtue,
I am affianc'd this man's wife as strongly   20
As words could make up vows; and, my good lord,
But Tuesday night last gone in 's garden-house
He knew me as a wife. As this is true,
Let me in safety raise me from my knees,
Or else for ever be confixed here,   25
A marble monument!

3 known had sexual relations with   **5 She** (As part of the grand plan, Isabella has just finished accusing Angelo licentious behavior. See V.i.97)
7 with . . . time with committing the offense at the very same time
8 depose swear, testify under oath   **9 effect** manifestations   **13 vow'd contract** (see III.i.213)   **14 fast belock'd** firmly bound by reason of vows

exchanged   **15 match** tryst (see III.i.243)   **16 supply thee** fulfill your
sexual desires   **17 her imagin'd** i.e., a likeness of her   **Noble Prince** (At
this point, Mariana resumes addressing the Duke.)   **20 affianc'd** betrothed
25 confixed firmly fixed

ALTERNATE
Isabella   [V.i.20–67]

THE MERCHANT OF VENICE

Bassanio wants in the worst way to travel to Belmont and court the heiress Portia, but he needs money to do so. Upon looking to his merchant friend Antonio for financial assistance, Bassanio learns that he too is cash-poor at the moment. Even so, Antonio manages to secure a loan from the moneylender Shylock—but only by agreeing to a most severe condition: if Antonio defaults, he must forfeit to Shylock a pound of his own flesh.

In Belmont, Portia is bound by her late father's will to marry the first suitor who can choose correctly from among three chests made of gold, silver, and lead, respectively. When Bassanio arrives on the scene, he quickly manages to succeed where all others before him have failed—the lead chest it is. Portia is elated by Bassanio's winning guess, and the two lovers are soon married.

Joy is short-lived, however, as word arrives that Antonio's ships have wrecked at sea; unable to repay the loan, the merchant is now faced with meeting Shylock's demand for a pound of his flesh. Bassanio rushes off to his friend's aid, followed shortly thereafter by Portia, who, disguised as a male lawyer, proves to be instrumental in saving Antonio's hide. In court it is determined that the conditions of Shylock's loan are not only pernicious, but virtually impossible to enforce. Antonio is thus spared (and so, it turns out, were his ships), while Shylock is sent off to a life of Christianity.

PORTIA, a rich heiress
NERISSA, a gentlewoman attending on Portia

PRINCE OF MOROCCO, suitor to Portia
ANTONIO, a merchant of Venice
BASSANIO, friend to Antonio, suitor to Portia
SHYLOCK, a Jewish moneylender
LAUNCELOT GOBBO, servant to Shylock
BALTHASAR, servant to Portia

(1)   PORTIA   [I.ii.10]

SCENE: Portia's house

{Portia is nearly at her wits' end. Her frustration stems from a provision of her late father's will, according to which she must marry the first suitor who can correctly choose from among three small chests adorned with gold, silver, and lead, respectively. But when her servant Nerissa attempts to console Portia with some well-intentioned words of wisdom, she will have none of it.}

1   Good sentences, Nerissa, and well pronounc'd. But, if to do were as easy as to know what to do, chapels had been churches and poor men's cottages princes' palaces. It is a good divine that follows his own instructions; I can easier teach twenty what were good to be done, than to be one of the twenty to follow
5   mine own teaching. The brain may devise laws for the blood, but a hot temper leaps o'er a cold decree—such a hare is madness the youth, to skip o'er the meshes of good counsel the cripple. But this reasoning is not in the fashion to choose me a husband. O me, the word "choose!" I may neither choose who I would nor refuse who I dislike; so is the will of a living daughter curb'd by the
10   will of a dead father. Is it not hard, Nerissa, that I cannot choose one nor refuse none? First, there is the Neapolitan prince: there's a colt indeed, for he doth nothing but talk of his horse; and he makes it a great appropriation to his own good parts that he can shoe him himself. I am much afeared my lady his mother play'd false with a smith. Then is there the County Palatine: he doth nothing
15   but frown, as who should say "An you will not have me, choose." He hears merry tales and smiles not. I fear he will prove the weeping philosopher when he grows old, being so full of unmannerly sadness in his youth. I had rather be married to a death's-head with a bone in his mouth than to either of these. God defend me from these two! [As for] the French lord, Monsieur Le Bon;
20   God made him, and therefore let him pass for a man. In truth, I know it is a sin to be a mocker—but he! Why, he hath a horse better than the Neapolitan's, a better bad habit of frowning than the Count Palatine; he is every man in no man. If a throstle sing, he falls straight a cap'ring. He will fence with his own shadow. If I should marry him, I should marry twenty husbands. If he would
25   despise me, I would forgive him, for if he love me to madness, I shall never requite him. Then to Falconbridge, the young Baron of England; you know I say nothing to him, for he understands not me, nor I him. He hath neither Latin, French, nor Italian, and you will come into the court and swear that I have a poor pennyworth in the English. He is a proper man's picture, but alas, who
30   can converse with a dumb-show? How oddly he is suited! I think he bought his doublet in Italy, his round hose in France, his bonnet in Germany, and his behavior everywhere. [And finally] the young German, the Duke of Saxony's nephew: when he is best, he is a little worse than a man, and when he is worst, he is little better than a beast. An the worst fall that ever fell, I hope I shall

make shift to go without him. [Indeed, Nerissa] I am glad this parcel of wooers   35
were so reasonable to return to their homes and to trouble me with no more
suit, for there is not one among them but I dote on his very absence, and I
pray God grant them a fair departure.

1 sentences maxims **pronounc'd** spoken   **3 divine** priest   **5 blood** (It
was thought at the time that the blood was the seat of passionate emotions.)
decree resolution   **7 meshes** nets (such as those used to ensnare hares)
good . . . cripple Wisdom the feeble old man   **in the fashion** of a kind to
help me   **10 hard** harsh, severe   **12 appropriation** addition   **14 false**
adulterously   **smith** blacksmith   **County** Count   **15 who should** if to   **An** if
choose i.e., then do as you like   **16 prove** turn out to be   **17 unmannerly**
unbecoming   **18 death's-head . . . mouth** skull and crossbones
23 throstle thrush   **falls . . . cap'ring** immediately starts prancing about
29 proper man's picture handsome man   **30 dumb-show** story enacted
without words   **suited** attired   **31 doublet** jacket-like upper garment   **hose**
tight-fitting pants   **bonnet** cap   **35 make shift** manage

(2)   PORTIA   [III.ii.1]

SCENE: Portia's house

{Though Bassanio has won Portia's heart, he's not yet won her father's game (see
previous entry). As Bassanio prepares to try his luck with the three chests, Portia
wonders if they might not wait a while, knowing as she does that an incorrect
guess means they must part forever.}

I pray you, tarry. Pause a day or two   1
Before you hazard; for, in choosing wrong,
I lose your company. Therefore forbear a while.
There's something tells me, but it is not love,
I would not lose you; and you know yourself,   5
Hate counsels not in such a quality.
But lest you should not understand me well—
And yet a maiden hath no tongue but thought—
I would detain you here some month or two
Before you venture for me. I could teach you   10
How to choose right, but then I am forsworn;
So will I never be. So may you miss me;
But if you do, you'll make me wish a sin,
That I had been forsworn. Beshrew your eyes;
They have o'erlook'd me and divided me!   15

One half of me is yours, the other half yours—
Mine own, I would say; but if mine, then yours,
And so all yours. O, these naughty times
Put bars between the owners and their rights!
20   And so, though yours, not yours. Prove it so,
Let fortune go to hell for it, not I.
I speak too long, but 'tis to peize the time,
To eche it and to draw it out in length,
To stay you from election.

I tarry wait   **2 hazard** venture a guess   **3 forbear** withdraw   **5 would not**
do not wish to   **6 quality** manner   **14 Beshrew** curse   **15 o'erlook'd**
bewitched   **18 naughty** wicked   **20 Prove it so** if such should prove to be
so   **22 peize** weigh down, retard   **23 eche it** eke it out   **24 stay** delay
election (making your) selection

(3)   PORTIA   [III.ii.149]

SCENE: Portia's house

*{By opting for the lead chest (see entry (1), above), Bassanio has won both the
game and Portia's hand in marriage. All that remains is for the lady to grant
him his just reward.}*

1   You see me, Lord Bassanio, where I stand,
Such as I am. Though for myself alone
I would not be ambitious in my wish,
To wish myself much better, yet for you
5   I would be trebled twenty times myself,
A thousand times more fair, ten thousand times
More rich, that only to stand high in your account,
I might in virtues, beauties, livings, friends,
Exceed account. But the full sum of me
10   Is sum of something, which, to term in gross,
Is an unlesson'd girl, unschool'd, unpracticed;
Happy in this, she is not yet so old
But she may learn; happier than this,
She is not bred so dull but she can learn;
15   Happiest of all is that her gentle spirit
Commits itself to yours to be directed,
As from her lord, her governor, her king.
Myself and what is mine to you and yours

Is now converted. But now I was the lord
Of this fair mansion, master of my servants,   20
Queen o'er myself; and even now, but now,
This house, these servants, and this same myself
Are yours, my lord's. I give them with this ring,
Which when you part from, lose, or give away,
Let it presage the ruin of your love   25
And be my vantage to exclaim on you.

4 myself i.e., that I were   **7 account** estimation, favor   **8 livings**
possessions   **9 account** calculation **full sum** sum total   **10 Is sum of** adds
up to   **term in gross** state in full   **12 Happy** fortunate   **14 dull** dense,
feebleminded   **17 from** by   **19 But now** moments ago   **21 even now,**
but now precisely now, just now   **25 ruin** decay   **26 vantage…on**
opportunity to reproach

(4)   PORTIA   [III.iv.45]

SCENE: Portia's house

{No sooner had they completed their wedding vows than Bassanio was com-
pelled to leave Portia and return to Venice. Now, not long after her husband's
departure, Portia's brainstorm has her and Nerissa hurriedly making their own
plans for travel to Venice.} [Though lines 1–12 can be deleted to avoid the
Balthasar complication, they are quite useful in establishing this piece's
energetic pace.]

Now, Balthasar,   1
As I have ever found thee honest-true,
So let me find thee still. Take this letter,
And use thou all th' endeavor of a man
In speed to Padua. See thou render this   5
Into my cousin's hands, Doctor Bellario,
And look what notes and garments he doth give thee.
Bring them, I pray thee, with imagin'd speed
Unto the traject, to the common ferry
Which trades to Venice. Waste no time in words,   10
But get thee gone. I shall be there before thee.
[*Balthasar exits.*]
Come on, Nerissa, I have work in hand
That you yet know not of. We'll see our husbands
Before they think of us; but in such a habit   15

That they shall think we are accomplished
With that we lack. I'll hold thee any wager,
When we are both accoutred like young men,
I'll prove the prettier fellow of the two,
20   And wear my dagger with the braver grace,
And speak between the change of man and boy
With a reed voice, and turn two mincing steps
Into a manly stride, and speak of frays
Like a fine bragging youth, and tell quaint lies,
25   How honorable ladies sought my love,
Which, I denying, they fell sick and died—
I could not do withal! Then I'll repent,
And wish, for all that, that I had not kill'd them.
And twenty of these puny lies I'll tell,
30   That men shall swear I have discontinued school
Above a twelvemonth. I have within my mind
A thousand raw tricks of these bragging Jacks,
Which I will practice.
But come, I'll tell thee all my whole device
35   When I am in my coach, which stays for us
At the park gate; and therefore haste away,
For we must measure twenty miles today.

5 Padua (Padua was famous as a center for the study of civil law.)
6 cousin's kinsman's   **8 imagin'd speed** speed as quick as thought
9 traject ferry   **10 trades** travels back and forth   **13 work in hand** a plan
underway   **14 our husbands** (Nerissa's new husband accompanied Bassanio
on his journey to Venice.)   **15 a habit** attire   **16 accomplished** equipped
17 that we lack what we lack (in the way of uniquely male characteristics)
hold offer   **20 braver** finer, more splendid   **21 change** (in vocal pitch)
24 quaint elaborate   **27 do withal** help it   **30 discontinued** not attended
31 Above for more than   **32 raw** vulgar, rude   **Jacks** knaves   **34 device**
plan   **35 stays** waits   **36 haste** hasten, hurry   **37 measure** cover, travel

ALTERNATE
Portia   [IV.i.184–205]

THE MERRY WIVES OF WINDSOR

In dire need of some cash, Falstaff decides to court Mistresses Ford and Page, hoping he can thereby gain access to their husbands' purses. The ladies are understandably revolted by Falstaff's amorous overtures, but decide to lead him on anyway just for the fun of it. Employing Mistress Quickly as their go-between, the two wives begin their intrigue by arranging separate assignations with the clueless Sir John.

Elsewhere, a disgruntled pair of Falstaff's followers have alerted Masters Ford and Page to Falstaff's designs on their wives. Unlike Page, Ford takes the warning to heart, but is frustrated in his two attempts to catch his wife and Sir John in the act.

After Mistresses Ford and Page finally inform one and all of their shenanigans with Falstaff, everyone agrees it would be swell to stage one last, elaborate humiliation of the fat knight. The plan comes off swimmingly, of course, and afterward the conspirators all saunter over to Page's house for a bit of country cheer.

MISTRESS FORD, wife to Ford
MISTRESS PAGE, wife to Page
MISTRESS QUICKLY, confidante to Mistresses Ford and Page

SIR JOHN FLASTAFF, a roguish knight
MASTER FORD, a gentleman of Windsor
MASTER PAGE, a gentleman of Windsor
SIR HUGH EVANS, a Welsh parson
NYM, follower of Falstaff
PISTOL, follower of Falstaff

(1)   MISTRESS PAGE   [II.i.i]

SCENE: Page's house

{Mistress Page has just received a laughable love letter from Falstaff. She is not amused.}

1   What, have I scap'd love-letters in the holiday-time of my beauty, and am I now
     a subject for them? Let me see: [*Reads the letter.*]
          "Ask me no reason why I love you; for though Love use Reason for his
     precisian, he admits him not for his counselor. You are not young, no more am I;
5   go to then, there's sympathy. You are merry, so am I; ha, ha—then there's more
     sympathy. You love sack, and so do I; would you desire better sympathy? Let it
     suffice thee, Mistress Page—at the least, if the love of soldier can suffice—that
     I love thee. I will not say, pity me—'tis not a soldier-like phrase—but I say, love
     me. By me,
10   Thine own true knight,
               By day or night,
               Or any kind of light,
               With all his might
               For thee to fight,
15   John Falstaff."
     What a Herod of Jewry is this! O wicked, wicked world! One that is well-nigh
     worn to pieces with age to show himself a young gallant! What an unweigh'd
     behavior hath this Flemish drunkard pick'd—with the devil's name!—out of
     my conversation, that he dares in this manner assay me? Why, he hath not
20   been thrice in my company! What should I say to him? I was then frugal of
     my mirth. Heaven forgive me! Why, I'll exhibit a bill in the parliament for the
     putting down of men. How shall I be reveng'd on him? For reveng'd I will be,
     as sure as his guts are made of puddings.

1 scap'd escaped **holiday-time** festive period, i.e., youthful days   **3 Love**
Cupid   **4 precisian** strict moral or religious advisor **counselor** practical
advisor   **5 sympathy** agreement, harmony   **6 sack** a white wine from Spain
16 Herod of Jewry i.e., a blustering tyrant (Herod was typically portrayed
in such a manner in the medieval mystery plays.)   **17 unweigh'd** rash
18 Flemish (The Flemish people were generally thought of as heavy
drinkers.) **with** in   **19 conversation** manner, behavior **assay** accost, make
amorous advances to   **20 should I say** could I possibly have said
21 exhibit present   **22 putting down** silencing, suppression
23 puddings a sausage-like concoction

(2)   **MISTRESS FORD**   **[II.1.41]**

SCENE: Page's house

{Out of breath and with a lascivious love letter of her own in hand (see preceding entry), Mistress Ford arrives at Page's home anxious to apprise her compatriot of this unfathomable event.}

O Mistress Page, give me some counsel! O woman, if it were not for one   1
trifling respect, I could come to such honor! If I would but go to hell for an
eternal moment or so, I could be knighted. [*Gives her the letter.*] I shall think
the worse of fat men, as long as I have an eye to make difference of men's
liking. And yet he would not swear; prais'd women's modesty; and gave such   5
orderly and well-behav'd reproof to all uncomliness, that I would have sworn
his disposition would have gone to the truth of his words. But they do no
more adhere and keep place together than the Hundredth Psalm to the tune
of "Greensleeves." What tempest, I trow, threw this whale, with so many tuns
of oil in his belly, ashore at Windsor? How shall I be reveng'd on him? I think   10
the best way were to entertain him with hope, till the wicked fire of lust have
melted him in his own grease. Did you ever hear the like?

4–5 make . . . liking tell the difference between men's physiques
6 uncomliness unseemly appearance or behavior   **7 disposition** nature
gone . . . truth supported, confirmed   **9 "Greensleeves"** (A popular love
song of the day.)   **trow** wonder   **tuns** a measure of liquid capacity, each
somewhere between 63–140 gallons   **11 entertain . . . hope** lead him on

(3)   **MISTRESS QUICKLY**   **[II.11.59]**

SCENE: A room in the Garter Inn

{Recruited by Mistresses Page and Ford to assist them in their plot of revenge against Falstaff, Quickly sets the plan in motion by rendezvousing with Sir John at this favorite pub.}

Marry, this is the short and the long of it: you have brought [Mistress Ford]   1
into such a canaries as 'tis wonderful. The best courtier of them all, when the
court lay at Windsor, could never have brought her to such a canary. Yet there
has been knights, and lords, and gentlemen with their coaches—I warrant you,
coach after coach, letter after letter, gift after gift; smelling so sweetly, all musk,   5
and so rushling, I warrant you, in silk and gold; and in such alligant terms, and
in such wine and sugar of the best and the fairest, that would have won any

woman's heart; and, I warrant you, they could never get an eye-wink of her.
I had myself twenty angels given me this morning; but I defy all angels, in any
10   such sort, as they say, but in the way of honesty; and, I warrant you, they could
never get her so much as sip on a cup with the proudest of them all. And yet
there has been earls, nay, which is more, pensioners; but, I warrant you, all is
one with her. [Yet now] she hath receiv'd your letter—for the which she thanks
you a thousand times—and she gives you to notify that her husband will be
15   absence from his house between ten and eleven. Then you may come and see
the picture, she says, that you wot of. Master Ford, her husband, will be from
home. Alas, the sweet woman leads an ill life with him. He's a very jealousy
man. She leads a very frampold life with him, good heart. But I have another
messenger to your worship. Mistress Page hath her hearty commendations to
20   you too; and let me tell you in your ear, she's as fartuous a civil modest wife,
and one, I tell you, that will not miss you morning nor evening prayer, as any
is in Windsor, whoe'er be the other. And she bade me tell your worship that
her husband is seldom from home, but she hopes there will come a time. I
never knew a woman so dote upon a man. Surely I think you have charms, la;
25   yes, in truth.

1 Marry indeed   **2 canaries** state of excitement (perhaps referring to a
lively sixteenth-century court dance called the "Canary")   **6 rushling**
rustling (i.e., dressed in a garment made of material that, when one moves
about, makes a rustling sound)   **alligant** (most likely Quickly's corruption of
"elegant")   **9 twenty angels** twenty gold coins bearing the image of an
angel   **given me** (i.e., as a fee to act as go-between)   **12 pensioners**
gentlemen serving as bodyguards to the sovereign within the grounds of the
royal palace   **14 to notify** notice   **15 absence** absent   **16 wot** know
18 frampold disagreeable   **19 messenger to** message for   **hearty**
heartfelt   **19 commendations** greetings   **20 fartuous** (Quickly's
corruption of "virtuous")   **civil** respectable   **modest** proper   **21 miss you**
miss   **24 have charms** weave magic spells

(4)   MISTRESS PAGE   [IV.iv.28]

SCENE: Ford's house

*{With her husband, the Fords, and Parson Evans all paying close attention,
Mistress Page lays out one final humiliation of the unscrupulous Falstaff. And
this time, everyone but the fat knight will be in on the fun.}*

1   There is an old tale goes that Herne the hunter,
Sometime a keeper here in Windsor forest,
Doth all the winter-time, at still midnight,

Walk round about an oak, with great ragg'd horns;
And there he blasts the tree, and takes the cattle,   5
And makes milch-kine yield blood, and shakes a chain
In a most hideous and dreadful manner.
You have heard of such a spirit, and well you know
The superstitious idle-headed eld
Receiv'd and did deliver to our age   10
This tale of Herne the hunter for a truth.
Marry, this is our device:
That Falstaff at that oak shall meet with us,
Disguis'd like Herne, with huge horns on his head.
Nan Page my daughter, and my little son,   15
And three or four more of their growth, we'll dress
Like urchins, ouphes, and fairies, green and white,
With rounds of waxen tapers on their heads,
And rattles in their hands. Upon a sudden,
As Falstaff, she, and I are newly met,   20
Let them from forth a sawpit rush at once
With some diffused song. Upon their sight,
We two in great amazedness will fly.
Then let them all encircle him about,
And, fairy-like, to pinch the unclean knight;   25
And ask him why, that hour of fairy revel,
In their so sacred paths he dares to tread
In shape profane. [Then] the truth being known,
We'll all present ourselves, dis-horn the spirit,
And mock him home to Windsor.   30

2 Sometime at one time   **3 still** silent   **4 ragg'd** pronged, jagged
5 blasts blights   **takes** bewitches   **6 milch-kine** milk cows   **9 eld** folk of
an earlier generation   **12 Marry** indeed   **16 growth** size, stature
17 urchins, ouphes interchangeable terms for goblins and elves
18 waxen tapers candles   **19 Upon a sudden** suddenly   **20 she**
(referring to Mistress Ford)   **21 sawpit** open pit over which wood was
sawed   **22 diffused** confused, wild

ALTERNATE
Mistress Quickly   [V.v.55–76]

A MIDSUMMER NIGHT'S DREAM

Helena loves Demetrius, but Demetrius only has eyes for Hermia. Hermia, on the other hand, has just run off with Lysander. Before long, all four lovers end up in a forest outside Athens.

In these very same woods reside the King and Queen of the Fairies, Oberon and Titania, who have recently locked horns over the services of a young boy. Determined that he shall be the one who employs the lad, Oberon manages to anoint Titania's eyes with a potion that will induce her to fall in love with the first creature she sees. If Oberon's plot unfolds as intended, Titania will be so humiliated she will be forced to relinquish the boy to him.

For good measure, Oberon instructs his servant, Puck, to similarly enchant Demetrius, whose heartless rejection of Helena the fairy King has just witnessed. Puck botches the job, however, and ends up sprinkling both Demetrius and Lysander with the potion, thereby inducing them to passionately pursue a bewildered Helena.

Meanwhile, a bewitched Titania is in hot pursuit herself. The object of her lust is a local simpleton named Bottom—this despite the fact that Bottom's head has of late been changed into that of an ass, courtesy of the impish Puck. Mayhem ensues, of course, until Oberon finally sets things right by releasing Lysander, Bottom, and Titania from their spells.

By story's end, marriages and merriment are everywhere, as one and all gather to enjoy an unforgettable performance of "Pyramus And Thisby," courtesy of Bottom and his fellow players.

HERMIA, in love with Lysander
HELENA, in love with Demetrius
TITANIA, Queen of the Fairies

THESEUS, Duke of Athens
LYSANDER, in love with Hermia
DEMETRIUS, in love with Hermia
BOTTOM, a weaver and would-be actor
OBERON, King of the Fairies
PUCK, aide to Oberon

(1)   HELENA   [I.i.226]

SCENE: Athens; the palace of Theseus

{Helena loves Demetrius, but Demetrius only has eyes for Hermia. With a moment to herself, Helena reflects upon this sad state of affairs, and the fickle ways of love.}

How happy some o'er other some can be!   1
Through Athens I am thought as fair as she.
But what of that? Demetrius thinks not so;
He will not know what all but he do know.
And as he errs, doting on Hermia's eyes,   5
So I, admiring of his qualities.
Things base and vile, holding no quantity,
Love can transpose to form and dignity.
Love looks not with the eyes, but with the mind,
And therefore is wing'd Cupid painted blind.   10
Nor hath Love's mind of any judgment taste;
Wings, and no eyes, figure unheedy haste.
And therefore is Love said to be a child,
Because in choice he is so oft beguil'd.
As waggish boys in game themselves forswear,   15
So the boy Love is perjur'd everywhere.
For ere Demetrius look'd on Hermia's eyne,
He hail'd down oaths that he was only mine;
And when this hail some heat from Hermia felt,
So he dissolv'd, and show'rs of oaths did melt.   20
I will go tell him of fair Hermia's flight.
Then to the wood will he tomorrow night
Pursue her; and for this intelligence
If I have thanks, it is a dear expense.
But herein mean I to enrich my pain,   25
To have his sight thither and back again.

1 some...be some people can be compared to other people   **2 Through** throughout   **6 admiring of** wondering at   **7 holding no quantity** lacking proportion, unshapely   **8 transpose** transform   **dignity** worth, value **11 hath...taste** has Love, which is founded on emotion, even a trace ("taste") of judgment or reason   **12 figure** symbolize   **unheedy** heedless, ill-advised   **15 waggish** roguish   **game** fun, jest   **16 perjur'd** forsworn **17 eyne** eyes   **21 flight** (see l.i.156)   **23 intelligence** information **24 dear expense** costly gain   **25 enrich** give value to   **26 his sight thither** the sight of him there

(2)   HELENA   [II.1.195]

SCENE: A wooded area near Athens

{Evidently, love is not only blind (see previous entry), but deaf as well. Helena is so infatuated with her beloved Demetrius that his rather unambiguous snub of the maid ("get thee gone, and follow me no more") fails to put her off in the least.}

1   You draw me, you hard-hearted adamant;
     But yet you draw not iron, for my heart
     Is true as steel. Leave you your power to draw,
     And I shall have no power to follow you.
5   I am your spaniel; and, Demetrius,
     The more you beat me, I will fawn on you.
     Use me but as your spaniel, spurn me, strike me,
     Neglect me, lose me; only give me leave,
     Unworthy as I am, to follow you.
10   What worser place can I beg in your love—
     And yet a place of high respect with me—
     Than to be used as you use your dog?
     The wildest beast hath not such a heart as you.
     Run when you will, the story shall be chang'd:
15   Apollo flies and Daphne holds the chase,
     The dove pursues the griffin, the mild hind
     Makes speed to catch the tiger—bootless speed,
     When cowardice pursues and valor flies.
     Fie, Demetrius!
20   Your wrongs do set a scandal on my sex.
     We cannot fight for love, as men may do;
     We should be woo'd, and were not made to woo.
     [Yet] I'll follow thee and make heaven of hell,
     To die upon the hand I love so well.

1 adamant magnetic stone (with a play on "hard-hearted," in that adamant was then considered the hardest of all substances)   **3 Leave** forsake, give up   **8 Neglect** ignore, disregard   **11 respect** regard   **15 Apollo . . . chase** (In the ancient myth it was Daphne who fled from Apollo; here, however, the story is "chang'd," and the female "holds the chase.")   **16 griffin** mythical creature with a lion's body and an eagle's head and wings   **mild** timid   **hind** female red deer   **17 bootless** unavailing, pointless   **19 Fie** (an expression of disgust)   **20 Your . . . sex** (i.e., because she, the female, must play the inappropriate role of pursuer)

(3)   HELENA   [III.II.192]

SCENE: A wooded area near Athens

*{Owing to mistaken identifications on Puck's part, both Lysander and Demetrius
have fallen under the influence of Oberon's love potion, and thus are both in hot
pursuit of Helena. Convinced that this sudden surplus of amorous attention is
nothing more than a cruel joke being played out at her expense, Helena confronts
the one she believes is behind it all—her one-time friend, Hermia.}*

Lo, she is one of this confederacy!   1
Now I perceive they have conjoin'd all three
To fashion this false sport, in spite of me.
Injurious Hermia, most ungrateful maid!
Have you conspir'd, have you with these contriv'd   5
To bait me with this foul derision?
Is all the counsel that we two have shar'd,
The sisters' vows, the hours that we have spent,
When we have chid the hasty-footed time
For parting us—O, is all forgot?   10
All school-days friendship, childhood innocence?
We, Hermia, like two artificial gods,
Have with our needles created both one flower,
Both on one sampler, sitting on one cushion,
Both warbling of one song, both in one key,   15
As if our hands, our sides, voices, and minds
Had been incorporate. So we grew together,
Like to a double cherry; seeming parted,
Bet yet a union in partition;
Two lovely berries molded on one stem.   20
So with two seeming bodies, but one heart;
Two of the first, like coats in heraldry,
Due but to one and crowned with one crest.
And will you rent our ancient love asunder,
To join with men in scorning your poor friend?   25
It is not friendly, 'tis not maidenly.
Our sex, as well as I, may chide you for it,
Though I alone do feel the injury.
Have you not set Lysander, as in scorn,
To follow me and praise my eyes and face?   30
And made your other love, Demetrius—
Who even but now did spurn me with his foot—
To call me goddess, nymph, divine and rare,

Precious, celestial? Wherefore speaks he this
35   To her he hates? And wherefore doth Lysander
Deny your love, so rich within his soul,
And tender me, forsooth, affection,
But by your setting on, by your consent?
What though I be not so in grace as you,
40   So hung upon with love, so fortunate,
But miserable most, to love unlov'd?
This you should pity rather than despise.
Ay, do! Persevere, counterfeit sad looks,
Make mouths upon me when I turn my back,
45   Wink at each other, hold the sweet jest up.
This sport, well carried, shall be chronicled.
If you have any pity, grace, or manners,
You would not make me such an argument.
But fare ye well. 'Tis partly my own fault,
50   Which death, or absence, soon shall remedy.

2 conjoin'd conspired together **5 contriv'd** plotted **6 bait** harass, torment **7 counsel** confidential talk **9 chid** chided, scolded **hasty-footed** quick-passing **12 artificial** creative **17 incorporate** of the same body **20 lovely** loving **21 seeming** external **22–23 Two...crest** i.e., we have two separate bodies... but just like two different coats of arms in heraldry that are crowned with a single crest, so are we united by one heart **24 rent** rend **32 spurn** kick **36 your love** his love for you **38 setting on** urging **39 What though** even though **in grace** favored, lucky **43 Persevere** keep it up **counterfeit** feign **sad** grave serious **44 mouths upon** faces at **45 hold...up** carry on the joke **46 well carried** successfully conducted **chronicled** written up in history books **48 argument** subject (of a prank)

ALTERNATES
Titania   [II.i.81–117]
Titania   [III.i.129–201]

MUCH ADO ABOUT NOTHING

Benedick is no fan of Beatrice, while Beatrice has little but scorn for Benedick. It's a bit surprising then that "friends" of each are soon conspiring to convince both Benedick and Beatrice that one is madly in love with the other.

Elsewhere in Messina, another plot unfolds. Because Don John resents the close friendship forged between his brother Don Pedro and young Claudio, he has decided to undermine Claudio's plans to marry Hero, daughter to Leonato.

Don John's scheme plays out precisely as planned when Claudio and Don Pedro happen to glimpse a servant disguised as Hero dallying with another man in Hero's bedroom window. Thus convinced that he's been betrayed by his betrothed, Claudio publicly humiliates Hero at the altar by refusing her hand in marriage.

Everything appears to have completely unraveled when, thanks in part to some dubious police work by Constable Dogberry, Don John's villainy is revealed and Claudio and Hero are reunited. As for Beatrice and Benedick, they eventually tumble to the fact that their would-be romance was founded on their friends' machinations, but even so resign themselves to the bonds of matrimony.

HERO, daughter to Leonato
BEATRICE, niece to Leonato
URSULA, a gentlewoman attending on Hero

DON PEDRO, Prince of Arragon
DON JOHN, bastard brother to Don Pedro
CLAUDIO, a young lord of Florence
BENEDICK, a young lord of Padua
LEONATO, governor of Messina
ANTONIO, brother to Leonato
DOGBERRY, a constable

(1)   **HERO**   [III.1.15]

SCENE: Leonato's orchard

*{Now that Benedick has been duped into thinking Beatrice loves him, the time
has come to play the flip side. With Hero and her attendant Ursula running
the show, part two of the elaborate ruse begins.}* [An abbreviated version of
this piece can be had by beginning with line 15 and/or ending with line 39.]

1	Now, Ursula, when Beatrice doth come,
	As we do trace this alley up and down,
	Our talk must only be of Benedick.
	When I do name him, let it be thy part
5	To praise him more than ever man did merit.
	My talk to thee must be how Benedick
	Is sick in love with Beatrice. Of this matter
	Is little Cupid's crafty arrow made,
	That only wounds by hearsay. Now begin:
10	[*Beatrice enters from behind.*]
	For look where Beatrice, like a lapwing, runs
	Close by the ground, to hear our conference.
	Now go we near her, that her ear lose nothing
	Of the false sweet bait that we lay for it.
15	[*They approach Beatrice's hiding place.*]
	No, truly, Ursula, she is too disdainful;
	I know her spirits are as coy and wild
	As haggards of the rock. Benedick deserves
	As much as may be yielded to a man;
20	But Nature never fram'd a woman's heart
	Of prouder stuff than that of Beatrice.
	Disdain and scorn ride sparkling in her eyes,
	Misprising what they look on, and her wit
	Values itself so highly that to her
25	All matter else seems weak. She cannot love,
	Nor take no shape nor project of affection,
	She is so self-endear'd. I never yet saw man,
	How wise, how noble, young, how rarely featur'd,
	But she would spell him backward. If fair-fac'd,
30	She would swear the gentleman should be her sister;
	If black, why, Nature, drawing of an antic,
	Made a foul blot; if tall, a lance ill-headed;
	If low, an agate very vilely cut;
	If speaking, why, a vane blown with all winds;
35	If silent, why, a block moved with none.

So turns she every man the wrong side out,
And never gives to truth and virtue that
Which simpleness and merit purchaseth.
No, not to be so odd, and from all fashions,
As Beatrice is, cannot be commendable.   40
But who dare tell her so? If I should speak,
She would mock me into air; O, she would laugh me
Out of myself, press me to death with wit.
Therefore let Benedick, like cover'd fire,
Consume away in sighs, waste inwardly.   45
It were a better death than die with mocks,
Which is as bad as die with tickling.
Rather I will go to Benedick
And counsel him to fight against his passion;
And truly, I'll devise some honest slanders   50
To stain my cousin with. One doth not know
How much an ill word may empoison liking.

2 trace traverse, walk   **9 That . . . hearsay** that wounds with mere rumor
11 lapwing a type of bird   **17 coy** haughty, insolent   **18 haggards** wild
female hawks   **20 fram'd** created   **23 Misprising** undervaluing   **25 All
matter else** anyone else's opinion   **26 take . . . affection** i.e., come to
grips with any conception of what love is   **28 How** no matter how **rarely**
unusually fine   **29 spell him backward** misconstrue him by seeing his
virtues as faults **fair-fac'd** fair of complexion   **31 black** dark complexioned
antic buffoon, grotesque figure   **33 agate** (alludes to the tiny figures cut
into agate for jewelry)   **38 simpleness** sincerity, integrity **purchaseth**
deserve   **39 from all fashions** contrary to all proper forms of behavior
42 into air i.e., until I was nothing   **43 press . . . death** (Pressing to death
with weights was a means of executing one who refused to enter a plea.)
44 cover'd fire a slow-burning fire kept beneath some form of protective
covering   **45 Consume . . . sighs** (Some believed that each sigh caused the
heart to lose a drop of blood.)   **50 honest** harmless (Hero intends to invent
mild slanders that will not besmirch Beatrice's character.)

ALTERNATE
Margaret   [III.iv.79–92]

OTHELLO

Othello and Desdemona fell in love and were secretly married, much to the chagrin of the bride's father, Brabantio. Othello's subsequent appearance before the Duke of Venice to defend his conduct is interrupted by news of an impending attack on Cyprus by the Turks. The Moor is sent to defend the island, and Desdemona is permitted to accompany him.

Enter Iago. Recently passed over for promotion to lieutenant in favor of the dashing Cassio, Iago vowed revenge on all concerned. Through a series of intricate machinations, he manages to make good on his word. First he secures Cassio's professional disgrace by getting the lieutenant drunk while on duty. Next, Iago contrives a plot to convince Othello that his wife and Cassio are having an affair.

While Cassio manages to survive an attempt on his life by Roderigo (a dupe of Iago's who also loves Desdemona), Othello's beloved wife is not so lucky. Consumed by jealousy, the Moor slinks into Desdemona's bedchamber and smothers her in her sleep.

When Iago's villainy is finally revealed, an enraged Othello attempts to slay him, but failing that, slays himself instead. Iago is then arrested and led off to his just rewards.

DESDEMONA, wife to Othello
EMILIA, wife to Iago

OTHELLO, a Moorish noble and officer
BRABANTIO, a senator, father to Desdemona
CASSIO, lieutenant to Othello
IAGO, ensign to Othello
RODERIGO, unsuccessful suitor to Desdemona

(1)   EMILIA   [IV.ii.115]

SCENE: A room in Othello's castle

{Iago's plot to poison Othello's mind is paying foul dividends. The Moor, convinced that his wife is stepping out on him, just stormed off after peppering poor Desdemona with a barrage of epithets. Now, an unsuspecting Emilia turns to her husband Iago for support. If only she knew... }

Alas, Iago, my lord hath so bewhor'd her,   1
Thrown such despite and heavy terms upon her,
That true hearts cannot bear it.
He call'd her whore. A beggar in his drink
Could not have laid such terms upon his callet.   5
Hath she forsook so many noble matches,
Her father and her country and her friends,
To be call'd whore? Hell gnaw his bones!
I will be hang'd if some eternal villain,
Some busy and insinuating rogue,   10
Some cogging, cozening slave, to get some office,
Have not devis'd this slander. I will be hang'd else.
Why should he call her whore? Who keeps her company?
What place? What time? What form? What likelihood?
The Moor's abus'd by some most villainous knave,   15
Some base notorious knave, some scurvy fellow.
O heaven, that such companions thou'dst unfold,
And put in every honest hand a whip
To lash the rascals naked through the world
Even from the east to the west!   20

1 bewhor'd her denounced her as a whore **2 despite** abuse **heavy**
harsh, hard **terms** epithets, names **5 callet** strumpet, whore **6 matches**
suitors **9 eternal** inveterate, unrepentant **10 busy** meddling **insinuating**
ingratiating **11 cogging** cheating **cozening** deceiving, defrauding
14 form set of circumstances **17 that** would that **unfold** expose, disclose

(2)   EMILIA   [IV.iii.68]

SCENE: A room in Othello's castle

{Ever the pragmatist, Emilia imparts to Desdemona a few of her thoughts on the subject of marital infidelity. First up: whether Emilia would betray her husband if offered "all the world" to do it.}

1   The world's a huge thing. It is a great price for a small vice. By my troth, I
think I should; and undo 't when I had done. Marry, I would not do such a thing
for a joint-ring, nor for measures of lawn, nor for gowns, petticoats, nor caps,
nor any petty exhibition; but, for all the whole world—'ud's pity, who would
5   not make her husband a cuckold to make him a monarch? I should venture
purgatory for 't. The wrong is but a wrong i' th' world; and having the world
for your labor, 'tis a wrong in your own world, and you might quickly make it
right.
But I do think it is their husband's faults
10   If wives do fall. Say that they slack their duties,
And pour our treasures into foreign laps;
Or else break out in peevish jealousies,
Throwing restraint upon us? Or say they strike us,
Or scant our former having in despite?
15   Why, we have galls; and though we have some grace,
Yet we have some revenge. Let husbands know
Their wives have sense like them. They see, and smell,
And have their palates both for sweet and sour,
As husbands have. What is it that they do
20   When they change us for others? Is it sport?
I think it is. And doth affection breed it?
I think it doth. Is 't frailty that thus errs?
It is so too. And have not we affections,
Desires for sport, and frailty, as men have?
25   Then let them use us well; else let them know,
The ills we do, their ills instruct us so.

1 By my troth (a mild oath affirming one's truthfulness)   **2 undo** reverse,
annul   **Marry** (a mild oath used to emphasize an assertion)   **3 joint-ring** a
type of inexpensive finger-ring that can be separated in half   **lawn** fine linen
4 exhibition gift   **'ud's pity** God's pity (a phrase of the day on the order of
"for God's sake")   **10 slack** neglect   **duties** marital responsibilities   **11 our
treasures** (refers to their husband's semen)   **foreign laps** i.e., other women
12 peevish childish   **13 restraint** confinement, restrictions   **14 scant...
despite** reduce our allowance just to spite us   **15 have galls** possess the
sort of spirit that resents wrongdoing or injustice   **17 sense like** the same
physical senses as   **20 change** exchange   **sport** a pleasant entertainment, an
amusing diversion   **21 affection** passion   **25 use** treat   **26 instruct us so**
serve as our example

ALTERNATE
Desdemona   [III.iv.122–154]

PERICLES

The trouble begins when Pericles realizes that the answer to a riddle posed by King Antiochus lies in the King's incestuous relationship with his daughter. Afraid of what having such knowledge might mean to his health, Pericles flees his native Tyre—landing first in Tharsus, before eventually settling in Pentapolis.

Shortly after marrying Thaisa, daughter to the King of Pentapolis, Pericles learns that Antiochus has died. Figuring it safe to return home, Pericles and the pregnant Thaisa set sail for Tyre. While at sea, Thaisa apparently dies while giving birth to a daughter, Marina. Thaisa's body is set adrift in a casket and eventually washes ashore in Ephesus, where wise old Cerimon manages to revive her. Pericles, meanwhile, stops by Tharsus to ask that Dionyza and Cleon raise his daughter Marina, and then continues on his way to Tyre.

Time passes, and the graces of an adolescent Marina come to so eclipse those of Dionyza's own daughter that Dionyza decides she must have Marina killed. But before the deed can be done, Marina is captured by pirates and ends up in a brothel in Mytilene. Rather than succumb there to a life of disrepute, Marina instead manages to become a noted teacher of the arts.

Eventually, Pericles and Marina find each other when Pericles happens to land in Mytilene. A vision Pericles has then compels him and Marina to travel to Ephesus, where the two are reunited with Thaisa, and everyone lives happily ever after.

DIONYZA, wife to Cleon
THAISA, wife to Pericles
MARINA, daughter to Pericles and Thaisa

ANTIOCHUS, King of Antioch
PERICLES, Prince of Tyre
CLEON, Governor of Tharsus
CERIMON, a lord of Ephesus

(1)   **DIONYZA**   [IV.III.I]

SCENE: The house of the Governor of Tharsus

{For many years, Cleon and Dionyza served as guardians to Pericles's daughter, Marina. Eventually, however, Dionyza became so jealous of the way in which her own daughter was outshone by Marina, that she arranged to have Marina murdered. When the time comes to defend her actions before an aghast Cleon, Dionyza is more than up to the task.}

1	Why, are you foolish? Can it be undone?
	I think you'll turn a child again.
	She is dead. Nurses are not the fates,
	To foster it, nor ever to preserve.
5	She died at night; I'll say so. Who can cross it?
	Unless you play the pious innocent,
	And for an honest attribute cry out
	"She died by foul play," [or] be one that thinks
	The petty wrens of Tharsus will fly hence
10	And open this to Pericles. I do shame
	To think of what a noble strain you are,
	And of how coward a spirit.
	None does know, but you, how she came dead;
	Nor none can know, Leonine being gone.
15	She did distain my child, and stood between
	Her and her fortunes. None would look on her,
	But cast their gazes on Marina's face,
	Whilst ours was blurted at and held a mawkin
	Not worth the time of day. It pierc'd me through.
20	And though you call my course unnatural—
	You not your child well loving—yet I find
	It greets me as an enterprise of kindness
	Perform'd to your sole daughter.
	And as for Pericles,
25	What should he say? We wept after her hearse,
	And yet we mourn. Her monument
	Is almost finished, and her epitaphs
	In glitt'ring golden characters express
	A general praise to her, and care in us
30	At whose expense 'tis done.
	You are like one that superstitiously
	Do swear to th' gods that winter kills the flies.
	But yet I know you'll do as I advise.

3 She (referring to Marina) **Nurses** guardians   **4 ever to preserve** to preserve (life) forever   **5 cross** contradict   **7 for** on account of **attribute** reputation   **9 petty wrens** (A superstition of the day held that concealed murders were revealed by tiny birds.)   **10 open** reveal **do shame** am ashamed   **14 Leonine** (It was to her servant Leonine that Dionyza assigned the task of murdering Marina. Dionyza later poisoned him, thereby concealing her complicity in the matter.)   **15 distain** sully, tarnish (i.e., cause to seem ugly by comparison)   **17 But** but only   **18 ours** our daughter's **blurted at** made light of, mocked **mawkin** slovenly girl, slut   **20 unnatural** devoid of human feeling, wicked   **22 greets** strikes, occurs to   **23 to** for   **26 yet** still   **29 general** universal, all-encompassing **care** consideration   **32 Do...
flies** (Though it's not certain precisely what Dionyza intends with this barb of hers, it's apparent that she is chiding her husband for being so fearful, comparing him to one who is so intimidated by divine justice that he swears to the gods that it was winter, and not he, who killed all the flies.)

ALTERNATE
Dionyza   [IV.i.1–51]

RICHARD II

Unable to settle a dispute between Bolingbroke and Mowbray concerning the Duke of Gloucester's murder, Richard instead elects to exile them. Mowbray is gone for good, while Bolingbroke is banished for six years.

Before long, however, Bolingbroke has returned to England—with a vengeance. His mission is to reclaim lands belonging to his family which Richard unduly seized upon the death of Bolingbroke's father, John of Gaunt.

Shortly after Richard arrives in Wales to squelch an Irish uprising, he learns of Bolingbroke's brazen reappearance on English soil. Fearing the worst, the King retires to nearby Flint Castle, where Bolingbroke and his army soon show up and take Richard into custody.

Once all concerned have resurfaced in London, Richard appears before Bolingbroke and agrees to relinquish the throne. After Bolingbroke is crowned King Henry IV, the new King makes known his desire to see the ex-King eliminated from the scene. Henry's implicit wish is granted when a band of assassins slip into Pomfret Castle and murder Richard in his cell.

DUCHESS OF GLOUCESTER, sister-in-law to John of Gaunt

KING RICHARD II
JOHN OF GAUNT, Duke of Lancaster, uncle to King Richard
BOLINGBROKE, Duke of Hereford, afterward King Henry IV
EARL OF NORTHUMBERLAND, an English noble in league with
     Bolingbroke
BISHOP OF CARLISLE

(1)   **DUCHESS OF GLOUCESTER**   [I.ii.9]

SCENE: The Duke of Lancaster's palace

{The Duke of Gloucester was recently executed under ambiguous circumstances. Because Gloucester's brother, John of Gaunt, neglected to avenge the Duke's death in a timely fashion, the Duchess of Gloucester has arrived at Gaunt's doorstep to make clear her disappointment.}

Finds brotherhood in thee no sharper spur?   1
Hath love in thy old blood no living fire?
Edward's seven sons, whereof thyself art one,
Were as seven vials of his sacred blood,
Or seven fair branches springing from one root.   5
Some of those seven are dried by nature's course,
Some of those branches by the Destinies cut;
But Thomas, my dear lord, my life, my Gloucester,
One vial full of Edward's sacred blood,
One flourishing branch of his most royal root,   10
Is crack'd, and all the precious liquor spilt,
Is hack'd down, and his summer leaves all faded,
By envy's hand and murder's bloody axe.
Ah, Gaunt, his blood was thine! That bed, that womb,
That metal, that self mold, that fashioned thee   15
Made him a man; and though thou livest and breathest,
Yet art thou slain in him. Thou dost consent
In some large measure to thy father's death,
In that thou seest thy wretched brother die,
Who was the model of thy father's life.   20
Call it not patience, Gaunt; it is despair.
In suff'ring thus thy brother to be slaught'red,
Thou showest the naked pathway to thy life,
Teaching stern murder how to butcher thee.
That which in mean men we entitle patience   25
Is pale cold cowardice in noble breasts.
What shall I say? To safeguard thine own life,
The best way is to venge my Gloucester's death.

1 spur incitement (to avenge Gloucester's life)   **3 Edward's** Edward III's (who preceded Richard as King of England)   **7 Destinies** Fates, goddesses of destiny   **8 Thomas** ("Thomas of Woodstock" is another of Gloucester's names.)   **13 envy's** malice's   **15 metal** substance of life   **self** very same   **19 wretched** unfortunate, woeful   **20 the model** in the image, a copy   **22 suff'ring** allowing, passively accepting   **23 naked** unguarded   **25 mean** common, lowly   **28 venge** avenge

RICHARD III

Though a bevy of would-be royal heirs stands between Richard and the throne of England, he is bound and determined to be the man who succeeds his ailing brother, King Edward IV. Even as Richard somehow manages to woo and wed the fair Lady Anne—this despite the fact that he killed her betrothed, the Prince of Wales—he embarks in earnest upon his plan to usurp the crown.

First of the potential successors to be eliminated from contention is Richard's brother the Duke of Clarence, who, at Richard's behest, is slain while imprisoned in the Tower of London. With Clarence out of the way, the death of King Edward enables Richard to finagle his way to the throne, which he quickly does through a series of subtle and not-so-subtle machinations.

To make sure he stays on top, Richard proceeds to tie up a few loose ends. For one thing, he sees to it that Edward's two young sons (and rightful heirs to the crown) are murdered. Next up: Richard's wife, Lady Anne, is neatly disposed of so that Richard can woo the late King Edward's daughter—a match that would further tighten his grip on the crown.

But when forces led by the Earl of Richmond arrive to do battle with the royal army at Bosworth Field, King Richard's day of reckoning comes at last. Richard's army goes down to defeat, while the King himself (sans horse) is slain by Richmond in hand-to-hand combat. The Wars of the Roses are finally over, and Richmond is hailed as King Henry VII.

QUEEN MARGARET, widow of King Henry VI

LADY ANNE, daughter-in-law to King Henry VI, afterward wife to Richard

KING EDWARD IV

GEORGE, DUKE OF CLARENCE, brother to Richard

RICHARD, DUKE OF GLOUCESTER, afterward King Richard III

HENRY, EARL OF RICHMOND, afterward King Henry VII

LORD STANLEY, an English noble

(1)   **LADY ANNE**   [I.ii.1]

SCENE: A street in London

{Lady Anne pauses for a moment of mourning, as she and a few guards escort the corpse of King Henry VI on its way from St. Paul's Cathedral to a nearby monastery.}

Set down, set down your honorable load—   1
If honor may be shrouded in a hearse—
Whilst I awhile obsequiously lament
Th' untimely fall of virtuous Lancaster.
Poor key-cold figure of a holy king,   5
Pale ashes of the house of Lancaster,
Thou bloodless remnant of that royal blood,
Be it lawful that I invocate thy ghost
To hear the lamentations of poor Anne,
Wife to thy Edward, to thy slaught'red son,   10
Stabb'd by the selfsame hand that made these wounds!
Lo, in these windows that let forth thy life,
I pour the helpless balm of my poor eyes.
O, cursed be the hand that made these holes!
Cursed the heart that had the heart to do it!   15
Cursed the blood that let this blood from hence!
More direful hap betide that hated wretch,
That makes us wretched by the death of thee,
Than I can wish to wolves, to spiders, toads,
Or any creeping venom'd thing that lives!   20
If ever he have child, abortive be it,
Prodigious, and untimely brought to light,
Whose ugly and unnatural aspect
May fright the hopeful mother at the view,
And that be heir to his unhappiness!   25
If ever he have wife, let her be made
More miserable by the life of him
Than I am made by my young lord and thee!
Come now towards Chertsey with your holy load,
Taken from Paul's to be interred there;   30
And still as you are weary of this weight,
Rest you, whiles I lament King Henry's corse.

3 obsequiously mournfully   **4 Lancaster** (Henry was of the House of
Lancaster.)   **5 key-cold** stone cold   **8 invocate** invoke, call forth
11 Stabb'd...wounds (see Henry VI, 3, V.v.41)   **12 windows** (referring to
his wounds)   **13 helpless balm** useless tears   **17 hap betide** fortune

befall **21 abortive** unnatural, freakish **22 Prodigious** abnormal, monstrous **25 his** i.e., Richard's **unhappiness** evil nature **28 by . . . thee** i.e., by the deaths of Prince Edward and King Henry VI, respectively **29 Chertsey** monastery near London where Henry's body is to be buried **31 still as** whenever **32 corse** corpse

(2)   LADY ANNE   [I.ii.43]

SCENE: A street in London

{Just as Lady Anne and the others are about to resume their excursion to Chertsey (see preceding entry), Richard appears and threatens to strike down one of the guards should he fail to halt this modest funeral procession. Lady Anne, for one, will not be intimidated.}

1   What do you tremble? Are you all afraid?
     Alas, I blame you not, for you are mortal,
     And mortal eyes cannot endure the devil.
     Avaunt, thou dreadful minister of hell!
5   Thou hadst but power over his mortal body;
     His soul thou canst not have. Therefore be gone
     Foul devil, for God's sake, and trouble us not;
     For thou hast made the happy earth thy hell,
     Fill'd it with cursing cries and deep exclaims.
10   If thou delight to view thy heinous deeds,
     Behold this pattern of thy butcheries.
     [*She uncovers the corpse.*]
     O gentlemen, see, see dead Henry's wounds
     Open their congeal'd mouths and bleed afresh!
15   Blush, blush, thou lump of foul deformity;
     For 'tis thy presence that exhales this blood
     From cold and empty veins where no blood dwells.
     Thy deeds inhuman and unnatural
     Provokes this deluge most unnatural.
20   O God, which this blood mad'st, revenge his death!
     O earth, which this blood drink'st, revenge his death!
     Either heav'n with lightning strike the murd'rer dead,
     Or earth gape open wide and eat him quick,
     As thou dost swallow up this good king's blood,
25   Which his hell-govern'd arm hath butchered!

   1 What why (Anne is addressing the guard who Richard has threatened.)
   4 Avaunt be gone **5 his** i.e., King Henry VI's **9 deep exclaims** heartfelt

exclamations   **11 pattern** sample   **14 bleed afresh** (Popular belief had it
that such a phenomenon occurred in the presence of the murderer.)
16 exhales draws forth   **18 unnatural** cruel, wicked   **19 unnatural**
supernatural   **23 quick** alive

(3)   QUEEN MARGARET   [I.III.187]

SCENE: The royal palace

*{Demonstrating that there yet remains a bit of fire in the old girl, Margaret drops
by the royal court to share a few sentiments with those who have contributed to
her downfall.}*

What? Were you snarling all before I came,   1
Ready to catch each other by the throat,
And turn you all your hatred now on me?
Did York's dread curse prevail so much with heaven
That Henry's death, my lovely Edward's death,   5
Their kingdom's loss, my woeful banishment,
Should all but answer for that peevish brat?
Can curses pierce the clouds and enter heaven?
Why then give way, dull clouds, to my quick curses!
Though not by war, by surfeit die your king,   10
As ours by murder, to make him a king!
Edward thy son, that now is Prince of Wales,
For Edward our son, that was Prince of Wales,
Die in his youth by like untimely violence!
Thyself a queen, for me that was a queen,   15
Outlive thy glory, like my wretched self!
Long mayst thou live to wail thy children's death,
And see another, as I see thee now,
Deck'd in thy rights, as thou art stall'd in mine!
Long die thy happy days before thy death,   20
And, after many length'ned hours of grief,
Die neither mother, wife, nor England's queen!
Rivers and Dorset, you were standers by,
And so wast thou, Lord Hastings, when my son
Was stabb'd with bloody daggers: God, I pray him   25
That none of you may live his natural age,
But by some unlook'd accident cut off!
And for thee, Gloucester,
If heaven have any grievous plague in store
Exceeding those that I can wish upon thee,   30

O, let them keep it till thy sins be ripe,
And then hurl down their indignation
On thee, the troubler of the poor world's peace!
The worm of conscience still begnaw thy soul!
35 Thy friends suspect for traitors while thou liv'st,
And take deep traitors for thy dearest friends!
No sleep close up that deadly eye of thine,
Unless it be while some tormenting dream
Affrights thee with a hell of ugly devils!
40 Thou elvish-mark'd, abortive, rooting hog!
Thou that wast seal'd in thy nativity
The slave of nature and the son of hell!
Thou slander of thy heavy mother's womb!
Thou loathed issue of thy father's loins!
45 Thou rag of honor, thou detested—Richard!

4 York's dread curse (see Henry VI, 3, I.iv.164–166) **7 answer for** equal, atone for **peevish brat** (referring to Rutland, Richard's deceased brother—see Henry VI, 3, I.iii) **9 quick** piercing **10 surfeit** an excessive lifestyle **12 thy** i.e., Queen Elizabeth's **14 like** the same **19 Deck'd** adorned **stall'd** installed **25 stabb'd ... daggers** (see Henry VI, 3, V.v.41) **God ... him** I pray to God **27 unlook'd** unforeseen **accident** incident, event **31 them** (referring to the heavens) **34 still** constantly **begnaw** gnaw at **35 Thy friends suspect** may you suspect your friends **36 deep** cunning, crafty **40 elvish-mark'd** scarred at birth by evil fairies **abortive** prematurely and unnaturally born **hog** (alludes to Richard's badge, featuring a wild boar) **41 seal'd** confirmed **42 slave of nature** i.e., as a result of his deformity **43 heavy** sorrowful

(4)   LADY ANNE   [IV.i.58]

SCENE: Before the Tower of London

{Though it's a bit late in the coming—she is, after all, about to be crowned the next Queen of England—Lady Anne finally recognizes and condemns the fickle ways that have brought her to this point.}

1   O, would to God that the inclusive verge
Of golden metal that must round my brow
Were red-hot steel, to sear me to the brains!
Anointed let me be with deadly venom,
5   And die, ere men can say, "God save the Queen!"
When he that is my husband now

Came to me as I follow'd Henry's corse;
When scarce the blood was well wash'd from his hands
Which issued from my other angel husband
And that dear saint which then I weeping follow'd— 10
O, when, I say, I look'd on Richard's face,
This was my wish: "Be thou," quoth I, "accurs'd
For making me, so young, so old a widow!
And when thou wed'st, let sorrow haunt thy bed;
And be thy wife—if any be so mad— 15
More miserable by the life of thee
Than thou hast made me by my dear lord's death!"
Lo, ere I can repeat this curse again,
Within so small a time, my woman's heart
Grossly grew captive to his honey words 20
And prov'd the subject of mine own soul's curse,
Which hitherto had held mine eyes from rest.
For never yet one hour in his bed
Did I enjoy the golden dew of sleep,
But with his timorous dreams was still awak'd. 25
Besides, he hates me for my father Warwick,
And will, no doubt, shortly be rid of me

1 inclusive verge enclosing rim (referring to the crown) **4 Anointed...
venom** (i.e., anointed with venom rather than with holy oil, which was a
traditional part of the coronation ceremony) **7 corse** corpse (see I.ii.1)
9 husband (referring to Prince Edward) **13 so...widow** live widowed for
so long **20 Grossly** stupidly **22 hitherto** thus far **25 timorous**
terrifying **still** constantly

ALTERNATES

Queen Margaret [IV.iv.35–115]
Duchess of York [IV.iv.166–196]

ROMEO AND JULIET

It's love at first sight when Romeo and Juliet meet during a masked ball being held in the house of Capulet—this despite the fact that their families are embroiled in a protracted blood feud. By the next afternoon, the two are secretly wed by Friar Laurence.

It's not long after that when a street fight ends tragically with Romeo's friend, Mercutio, dead at the hands of Juliet's cousin, Tybalt—who in turn is then slain by Romeo. For his part in the brawl, Romeo is banished, and after spending the night with his new bride, he retreats to the nearby city of Mantua.

Meanwhile, unaware of his daughter's recent elopement, Capulet has arranged for Juliet to marry a young nobleman named Paris. When Juliet's resistance to the idea is overruled by her insistent parents, the desperate newlywed turns to Friar Laurence for help. The Friar's solution is to provide Juliet with a potion that will make her appear dead for forty-two hours. If all goes as planned, Romeo will arrive at the Capulet burial vault shortly after Juliet is laid to rest, and spirit her away from Verona.

But alas, all does not go as planned. Because a messenger fails to reach Romeo with word of the Friar's scheme, Romeo arrives at Juliet's tomb believing that she has actually died. No sooner does Romeo imbibe a lethal potion he had earlier procured, than Juliet awakens. Discovering her dead husband beside her, Juliet stabs herself, and dies.

LADY CAPULET, mother to Juliet, wife to Capulet

JULIET, daughter to Capulet

NURSE, nurse to Juliet

ESCALUS, Prince of Verona

PARIS, a young noble of Verona

CAPULET, head of the house of Capulet

ROMEO, a young gentleman of Verona

MERCUTIO, friend to Romeo, kinsman to the Prince

BENVOLIO, cousin and friend to Romeo

TYBALT, cousin to Juliet

FRIAR LAURENCE, a Franciscan, confidant to Romeo and Juliet

(1) **NURSE** **[I.III.II]**

SCENE: A room in Capulet's house

{When Juliet's mother offers a simple observation ("Thou knowest my daughter's of a pretty age"), Nurse reciprocates with a reply that's far more than Lady Capulet had bargained for.}

Faith, I can tell her age unto an hour.   1
I'll lay fourteen of my teeth—and yet, to my teen
Be it spoken, I have but four—she's not fourteen.
How long is it now to Lammas-tide?
Come Lammas-eve at night shall she be fourteen.   5
Susan and she—God rest all Christian souls!—
Were of an age. Well, Susan is with God;
She was too good for me. But as I said,
On Lammas-eve at night shall she be fourteen,
That shall she, marry, I remember it well.   10
'Tis since the earthquake now eleven years,
And she was wean'd—I never shall forget it—
Of all the days of the year, upon that day;
For I had then laid wormwood to my dug,
Sitting in the sun under the dove-house wall.   15
My lord and you were then at Mantua—
Nay, I do bear a brain—but as I said,
When it did taste the wormwood on the nipple
Of my dug and felt it bitter, pretty fool,
To see it tetchy and fall out with the dug!   20
"Shake," quoth the dove-house; 'twas no need, I trow,
To bid me trudge!
And since that time it is eleven years,
For then she could stand high-lone; nay, by th' rood,
She could have run and waddled all about;   25
For even the day before, she broke her brow,
And then my husband—God be with his soul!—
'A was a merry man—took up the child.
"Yea," quoth he, "dost thou fall upon thy face?
Thou wilt fall backward when thou hast more wit,   30
Wilt thou not, Jule?" and, by my holidam,
The pretty wretch left crying and said "Ay."
To see now how a jest shall come about!
I warrant, an I should live a thousand years,
I never should forget it. "Wilt thou not, Jule?" quoth he,   35
And, pretty fool, it stinted and said "Ay."
And yet, I warrant, it had upon it brow

A bump as big as a young cock'rel's stone—
A perilous knock—and it cried bitterly.
40   "Yea," quoth my husband, "Fall'st upon thy face?
Thou wilt fall backward when thou comest to age,
Wilt thou not, Jule?" It stinted and said "Ay."
Peace, I have done. God mark thee to his grace!
Thou wast the prettiest babe that e'er I nurs'd.
45   An I might live to see thee married once,
I have my wish.

2 teen sorrow   **4 Lammas-tide** the days around the first of August
6 Susan Nurse's own child, who is no longer living   **7 an** a similar
10 marry (a mild oath used to emphasize a point)   **14 wormwood** a
bitter-tasting herb used to wean an infant **dug** breast   **17 bear a brain** have
a good memory   **19 fool** (used here as a term of endearment)   **20 tetchy**
peevish   **21 "Shake"...dove-house** i.e., with its sudden shaking due to
the earthquake (see line 11), the dove-house suggested to her it was time to
go   **trow** dare say, assure you   **22 trudge** move quickly   **24 high-lone** on
her feet without aid   **rood** cross   **26 broke her brow** bruised her forehead
(by falling down)   **28 'A** he   **took** picked   **30 wit** intelligence   **31 by my**
holidam (a mild oath of the day)   **33 come about** come true   **34 an** if
36 it she   **stinted** stopped (crying)   **37 it brow** its brow   **38 cock'rel's**
stone rooster's testicle   **43 I have done** I'm finished   **mark** commit
44 Thou (Nurse is addressing Juliet.)

(2)   JULIET   [II.ii.85]

SCENE: Capulet's orchard

{Moments ago Juliet was on her balcony unabashedly professing her love for
Romeo, oblivious to the fact that the object of her desire was at that moment
hiding among the trees below. It's no surprise, then, that when Romeo steps
forward to make his presence known, Juliet fears she may have unwittingly
played her hand too soon.}

1   Thou knowest the mask of night is on my face,
Else would a maiden blush bepaint my cheek
For that which thou hast heard me speak tonight.
Fain would I dwell on form; fain, fain deny
5   What I have spoke; but farewell compliment!
Dost thou love me? I know thou wilt say "Ay,"
And I will take thy word. Yet if thou swear'st,

Thou mayst prove false. At lovers' perjuries,
They say Jove laughs. O gentle Romeo,
If thou dost love, pronounce it faithfully;   10
Or if thou thinkest I am too quickly won,
I'll frown and be perverse and say thee nay,
So thou wilt woo; but else, not for the world.
In truth, fair Montague, I am too fond,
And therefore thou mayst think my behavior light.   15
But trust me, gentleman, I'll prove more true
Than those that have more coying to be strange.
I should have been more strange, I must confess,
But that thou overheard'st, ere I was ware,
My true-love passion. Therefore pardon me,   20
And not impute this yielding to light love,
Which the dark night hath so discovered.
Sweet, good night!
This bud of love, by summer's ripening breath,
May prove a beauteous flow'r when next we meet.   25
Good night, good night! As sweet repose and rest
Come to thy heart as that within my breast!

4 Fain gladly **form** ceremony   **5 compliment** social convention
8 mayst might   **12 perverse** petulant, contrary   **13 So thou wilt** in
order to have you   **else** otherwise   **14 fond** eager   **15 light** frivolous
17 coying coyness, affected modesty   **strange** aloof   **19 But** except   **ware**
aware (of you)   **21 not** do not   **impute** attribute   **22 discovered**
uncovered, revealed

(3)   **JULIET**   [III.ii.1]

SCENE: A room in Capulet's house

{An impatient Juliet awaits the coming of night—and with it the arrival of her husband.}

Gallop apace, you fiery-footed steeds,   1
Towards Phoebus' lodging! Such a wagoner
As Phaethon would whip you to the west,
And bring in cloudy night immediately.
Spread thy close curtain, love-performing night,   5
That runaways' eyes may wink, and Romeo
Leap to these arms, untalk'd of and unseen.

Lovers can see to do their amorous rites
By their own beauties; or, if love be blind,
10   It best agrees with night. Come, civil night,
Thou sober-suited matron, all in black,
And learn me how to lose a winning match,
Play'd for a pair of stainless maidenhoods.
Hood my unmann'd blood, bating in my cheeks,
15   With thy black mantle; till strange love grow bold,
Think true love acted simple modesty.
Come, night; come, Romeo; come, thou day in night;
For thou wilt lie upon the wings of night
Whiter than new snow upon a raven's back.
20   Come, gentle night; come, loving, black-brow'd night;
Give me my Romeo; and, when he shall die,
Take him and cut him out in little stars,
And he will make the face of heaven so fine
That all the world will be in love with night
25   And pay no worship to the garish sun.
O, I have bought the mansion of a love,
But not possess'd it, and, though I am sold,
Not yet enjoy'd. So tedious is this day
As is the night before some festival
30   To an impatient child that hath new robes
And may not wear them. O, here comes my nurse,
And she brings news; and every tongue that speaks
But Romeo's name speaks heavenly eloquence.
Now, nurse, what news?

1 apace swiftly **steeds** (referring to the horses that pull the sun god's chariot) **2 Phoebus** Apollo, the sun god **lodging** i.e., where the sun rests in the west **2–3 wagoner As Phaethon** i.e., speedy charioteer like Phaethon (Permitted to drive for a day the chariot of the sun, Phaethon proved unable to prevent the steeds from racing along at a breakneck pace.) **5 close** concealing **love-performing** abetting the deeds of love **6 runaways'** vagabond's, fugitive's **wink** close (with sleep) **10 civil** restrained, somber **11 sober-suited** soberly dressed **12 learn** teach **13 maidenhoods** (referring to both her and Romeo's virginities) **14 Hood . . . unmann'd, bating** (All are terms associated with the sport of falconry, here sporting double meanings. One covers ["hoods"] an untamed ["unmann'd"] bird in order to keep it from beating its wings ["bating"] in an attempt to escape. Juliet is thus asking nightfall to hide ["hood"] what would otherwise be evident; that she is sexually inexperienced ["unmann'd"] and that her cheeks are flush with fluttering ["bating"] blood.) **15 strange** shy, reserved **16 Think** and think **modesty** chastity **20 black-brow'd** dark complexioned

(4)   **JULIET**   [III.ii.97]

SCENE: A room in Capulet's house

{When Nurse informs Juliet of the hostile encounter between Tybalt and Romeo—a brawl that ended in her cousin's death and her husband's banishment—Juliet's initial reaction is to grieve for the former and curse the latter. Within moments, though, her sentiments are signaling for a 180-degree turn.}

Shall I speak ill of him that is my husband?   1
Ah, poor my lord, what tongue shall smooth thy name
When I, thy three-hours wife, have mangled it?
But wherefore, villain, didst thou kill my cousin?
That villain cousin would have kill'd my husband.   5
Back, foolish tears, back to your native spring;
Your tributary drops belong to woe,
Which you, mistaking, offer up to joy.
My husband lives, that Tybalt would have slain,
And Tybalt's dead, that would have slain my husband.   10
All this is comfort; wherefore weep I then?
Some word there was, worser than Tybalt's death,
That murd'red me. I would forget it fain,
But, O, it presses to my memory
Like damned guilty deeds to sinners' minds;   15
"Tybalt is dead, and Romeo—banished."
That "banished," that one word "banished,"
Hath slain ten thousand Tybalts. Tybalt's death,
Was woe enough, if it had ended there;
Or, if sour woe delights in fellowship   20
And needly will be rank'd with other griefs,
Why followed not, when she said "Tybalt's dead,"
Thy father, or thy mother, nay, or both,
Which modern lamentation might have moved?
But with a rearward following Tybalt's death,   25
"Romeo is banished," to speak that word,
Is father, mother, Tybalt, Romeo, Juliet,
All slain, all dead. "Romeo is banished!"
There is no end, no limit, measure, bound,
In that word's death; no words can that woe sound.   30

2 smooth speak well of   **3 three-hour's wife** (Juliet and Romeo were secretly wed earlier that afternoon.)   **7 Your...woe** your tears should be offered on some truly woeful occasion   **8 mistaking** misjudging (this occasion as some woeful event)   **joy** i.e., the joyous fact that Romeo still lives

11 comfort comforting news   **13 fain** gladly   **14 presses** pushes its way
21 needly of necessity   **rank'd with** included within a series of   **23 or both**
(are dead as well)   **24 Which . . . moved** which might have induced more
ordinary grief   **25 rearward** rear-guard (the second wave of an attacking
army)   **30 that woe sound** express or measure the depth of that woe

(5)   JULIET   [IV.III.14]

SCENE: Juliet's bedchamber

*{Juliet is alone, having just bid goodnight to her mother and Nurse. With both
a vial of sleeping potion and her dagger at hand, the time has come to set Friar
Laurence's plan into motion.}*

1	Farewell! God knows when we shall meet again.
	I have a faint cold fear thrills through my veins,
	That almost freezes up the heat of life.
	I'll call them back again to comfort me.
5	Nurse!—What should she do here?
	My dismal scene I needs must act alone.
	Come, vial. [*Takes out the vial.*]
	What if this mixture do not work at all?
	Shall I be married then tomorrow morning?
10	No, no, this shall forbid it. Lie thou there.
	[*She lays aside the dagger.*]
	What if it be a poison, which the friar
	Subtly hath minist'red to have me dead,
	Lest in this marriage he should be dishonor'd
15	Because he married me before to Romeo?
	I fear it is; and yet methinks it should not,
	For he hath still been tried a holy man.
	How if, when I am laid into the tomb,
	I wake before the time that Romeo
20	Come to redeem me? There's a fearful point!
	Shall I not then be stifled in the vault,
	To whose foul mouth no healthsome air breathes in,
	And there die strangled ere my Romeo comes?
	Or, if I live, is it not very like,
25	The horrible conceit of death and night,
	Together with the terror of the place—
	As in a vault, an ancient receptacle,
	Where, for this many hundred years, the bones
	Of all my buried ancestors are pack'd;

Where bloody Tybalt, yet but green in earth,   30
Lies fest'ring in his shroud; where, as they say,
At some hours in the night spirits resort—
Alack, alack, it is not like that I,
So early waking, what with loathsome smells,
And shrieks like mandrakes' torn out of the earth,   35
That living mortals, hearing them, run mad—
O, if I wake, shall I not be distraught,
Environed with all these hideous fears,
And madly play with my forefathers' joints,
And pluck the mangled Tybalt from his shroud,   40
And in this rage, with some great kinsman's bone,
As with a club, dash out my desp'rate brains?
O, look! Methinks I see my cousin's ghost
Seeking out Romeo, that did spit his body
Upon a rapier's point. Stay, Tybalt, stay!   45
Romeo, Romeo, Romeo! Here's drink—I drink to thee.
[*She takes up the vial, and drinks.*]

I we (referring to her, Nurse, and Lady Capulet)   **2 thrills** that shivers
6 act act out   **9 married** (Juliet refers to the marriage planned between
her and Paris that is scheduled to take place the next day.)   **13 Subtly** slyly
16 methinks it seems to me   **not** not be (a poison)   **17 still** always   **tried**
proved to be   **18 How** what   **20 redeem** save, rescue   **fearful** frightening
22 healthsome wholesome, healthy   **24 like** likely   **25 conceit** concept,
idea   **27 As in** inasmuch as it's   **30 green in earth** freshly buried
33 Alack (an exclamation of despair)   **35 shrieks...earth** (The mandrake
root often has a vague manlike shape, and as such was at one time credited
with displaying certain human behaviors—including the tendency to shriek
whenever it was uprooted.)   **36 That** so that   **38 Environed with**
surrounded by   **fears** objects of dread   **40 mangled** lacerated, wounded
44 spit impale   **45 Stay** stop

THE TAMING OF THE SHREW

Baptista has declared that, despite her many suitors, his younger daughter Bianca can be courted only after his older, shrewish one, Katharina, is first married off.

Attracted by the prospect of her sizable dowry, Petruchio gamely embraces the challenge of wooing Kate. A series of fiery confrontations between the two ensue, until Petruchio at last manages to both wed and tame the recalcitrant Kate.

KATHARINA, daughter to Baptista
BIANCA, daughter to Baptista

BAPTISTA, a rich gentleman of Padua
LUCENTIO, a young gentleman of Pisa, suitor to Bianca
PETRUCHIO, a gentleman of Verona, suitor to Katharina
GRUMIO, servant to Petruchio

(1) **KATHARINA** [V.II.136]

SCENE: Lucentio's house

{The metamorphosis of Katharina from rebellious shrew to dutiful wife appears to be complete. When two newlywed wives refuse to do their husbands' bidding, Petruchio instructs Kate to inform the ladies of the "duty they do owe their lords and husbands." Without hesitation, Katharina complies.}

1 Fie, fie! Unknit that threatening unkind brow,
And dart not scornful glances from those eyes
To wound thy lord, thy king, thy governor.
It blots thy beauty as frosts do bite the meads,
5 Confounds thy fame as whirlwinds shake fair buds,
And in no sense is meet or amiable.
A woman mov'd is like a fountain troubled;
Muddy, ill-seeming, thick, bereft of beauty.
And while it is so, none so dry or thirsty

Will deign to sip or touch one drop of it.   10
Thy husband is thy lord, thy life, thy keeper,
Thy head, thy sovereign; one that cares for thee,
And for thy maintenance commits his body
To painful labor both by sea and land,
To watch the night in storms, the day in cold,   15
Whilst thou li'st warm at home, secure and safe;
And craves no other tribute at thy hands
But love, fair looks, and true obedience—
Too little payment for so great a debt.
Such duty as the subject owes the prince,   20
Even such a woman oweth to her husband;
And when she is froward, peevish, sullen, sour,
And not obedient to his honest will,
What is she but a foul contending rebel
And graceless traitor to her loving lord?   25
I am asham'd that women are so simple
To offer war where they should kneel for peace,
Or seek for rule, supremacy, and sway,
When they are bound to serve, love and obey.
Why are our bodies soft and weak and smooth,   30
Unapt to toil and trouble in the world,
But that our soft conditions and our hearts
Should well agree with our external parts?
Come, come, you froward and unable worms!
My mind hath been as big as one of yours,   35
My heart as great, my reason haply more,
To bandy word for word and frown for frown;
But now I see our lances are but straws,
Our strength as weak, our weakness past compare,
That seeming to be most which we indeed least are.   40
Then vail your stomachs, for it is no boot,
And place your hands below your husband's foot;
In token of which duty, if he please,
My hand is ready, may it do him ease.

4 meads meadows   **5 Confounds thy fame** ruins your reputation
6 meet proper   **7 mov'd** angry   **troubled** agitated   **8 thick** muddled
15 watch keep watch   **18 fair** kind   **21 Even such** just as much
22 froward defiant, disobedient   **peevish** obstinate   **23 honest** honorable,
decent   **25 graceless** disrespectful   **26 simple** foolish   **29 bound**
obliged   **31 Unapt** unfit   **32 conditions** characteristics, qualities
34 unable impotent, weak   **35 big** haughty   **36 haply** perhaps   **41 vail**
humble   **stomachs** arrogant spirits   **no boot** of no use   **44 do him ease**
give him pleasure

THE TEMPEST

Twelve years ago, Prospero was ousted as the Duke of Milan by his brother Antonio, and set adrift at sea along with his baby daughter, Miranda. The two castaways eventually washed up on a remote island inhabited only by a cantankerous creature named Caliban. It is there that Prospero, as possessor of strange and supernatural powers, now prepares to exact his revenge.

A storm worked up by Prospero has shipwrecked the King of Naples and his company (including Prospero's brother Antonio) on the island. With the assistance of Ariel, his indentured spirit, Prospero proceeds to conjure a series of wondrous spectacles, all of which serve to thoroughly confound Antonio and the others. Once he's made his point, Prospero takes pity on his bewildered guests, provides them with safe passage to Naples, renounces his magic and grants Ariel his freedom.

MIRANDA, daughter to Prospero
ARIEL, an airy spirit

ALONSO, King of Naples
SEBASTIAN, brother to Alonso
PROSPERO, the rightful Duke of Milan
ANTONIO, brother to Prospero, the usurping Duke of Milan
CALIBAN, a savage, slave to Prospero
TRINCULO, a jester

(1)   ARIEL   [III.III.53]

SCENE: Somewhere on Prospero's island

{Per Prospero's bidding, Ariel pops up in the form of a "harpy"—a menacing beast of womanly face and vulture-like claws and wings—and proceeds to lecture Alonso and the others on the error of their ways.} [Though generally referred to in the masculine, Ariel is frequently portrayed by female actors—an approach that is particularly appropriate here, in light of the character's disguise.]

You are three men of sin, whom Destiny,   1
That hath to instrument this lower world
And what is in 't, the never-surfeited sea
Hath caus'd to belch up you, and on this island
Where man doth not inhabit—you 'mongst men   5
Being most unfit to live. I have made you mad;
And even with such-like valor men hang and drown
Their proper selves.
[*Alonso, Sebastian, and Antonio draw their swords.*]
You fools! I and my fellows
Are ministers of Fate. The elements,   10
Of whom your swords are temper'd, may as well
Wound the loud winds, or with bemock'd-at stabs
Kill the still-closing waters, as diminish
One dowle that's in my plume. My fellow-ministers   15
Are like invulnerable. If you could hurt,
Your swords are now too massy for your strengths
And will not be uplifted. But remember—
For that's my business to you—that you three
From Milan did supplant good Prospero;
Expos'd unto the sea, which hath requit it,   20
Him and his innocent child; for which foul deed
The pow'rs, delaying, not forgetting, have
Incens'd the seas and shores, yea, all the creatures,
Against your peace. Thee of thy son, Alonso,
They have bereft; and do pronounce by me   25
Ling'ring perdition, worse than any death
Can be at once, shall step by step attend
You and your ways; whose wraths to guard you from—
Which here, in this most desolate isle, else falls
Upon your heads—is nothing but heart's sorrow   30
And a clear life ensuing.

1 three men i.e., Alonso, Sebastian, and Antonio   **2 to** as its   **7 such-like valor** i.e., valor born of madness (as opposed to true courage)   **8 proper** own   **10 fellows** fellow spirits   **12 whom** which   **13 bemock'd-at** ridiculed, mocked at   **14 still-closing** always closing whenever parted   **15 dowle** tiny feather   **16 like** likewise **If** even if   **17 massy** heavy, massive   **21 hath requit it** has since repaid the deed (by belching you up here)   **26 bereft** taken away, deprived   **27 perdition** ruin   **29 whose** (refers to the heavenly "pow'rs" of line 23)   **31 is … sorrow** there is no way except through repentance   **32 clear** blameless, pure

ALTERNATE

Iris   [IV.i.60–75]

TITUS ANDRONICUS

Titus has returned to Rome from a successful military campaign against the Goths. With him are Tamora, Queen of the Goths, and her three sons, one of whom Titus sacrifices in retribution for his own two sons lost in battle. Though he is clearly the people's choice as Rome's next emperor, Titus defers in favor of the late Emperor's eldest son, Saturninus. In turn, Saturninus agrees to marry Titus's daughter, Lavinia—a plan that does not sit well with Saturninus's brother Bassianus, who claims Lavinia as his own betrothed.

A struggle ensues and Bassianus escapes with Lavinia, after which Saturninus opts for the beguiling Tamora as his new bride. Though Saturninus holds Titus responsible for this embarrassing turn of events, he is persuaded by Tamora to feign forgiveness for the time being, so that she might later "find a day to massacre them all."

Tamora's plot of revenge quickly takes shape. She and her sons, Chiron and Demetrius, encounter Bassianus and Lavinia out in the forest, where the former is murdered and the latter is raped and mutilated. When false evidence fabricated by Tamora's lover, Aaron, implicates Titus's sons Martius and Quintus in the murder of Bassianus, the two are quickly executed.

Things then turn from bad to worse for Titus when he discovers the pitiful Lavinia, mangled and mute. With Marcus and Lucius by his side, Titus plots his revenge.

The climactic carnage unfolds as everyone gathers for a banquet at Titus's home. A pie featuring the remains of Chiron and Demetrius (freshly butchered by Titus a bit earlier in the day) is served to Tamora, and for dessert she is stabbed to death. Titus slays poor Lavinia as well (the idea being that her shame dies with her), after which he is slain by Saturninus, who then is killed by Lucius. Since Lucius is the last one standing, he is proclaimed Rome's new Emperor, and promptly condemns Aaron to death by burial and starvation.

TAMORA, Queen of the Goths, wife to Saturninus
LAVINIA, daughter to Titus Andronicus, in love with Bassianus

SATURNINUS, Emperor of Rome
BASSIANUS, brother to Saturninus
TITUS ANDRONICUS, a Roman noble and general

MARCUS ANDRONICUS, brother to Titus Andronicus
LUCIUS, son to Titus Andronicus
DEMETRIUS, son to Tamora
CHIRON, son to Tamora
AARON, a Moor, beloved of Tamora

(1)   **TAMORA**   [I.1.428]

SCENE: Inside Rome's Senate House

{Tamora may be evil incarnate, but she's nobody's fool. Sensing that now is not the time to be chastising the wildly popular Titus or his sons for their role in Lavinia's "abduction," she pleads with her new husband, Saturninus, to let bygones be bygones... for now.}

1   My worthy lord, if ever Tamora
      Were gracious in those princely eyes of thine,
      Then hear me speak indifferently for all;
      And at my suit, sweet, pardon what is past.
5   My lord, the gods of Rome forfend
      I should be author to dishonor you.
      But on mine honor dare I undertake
      For good Lord Titus' innocence in all,
      Whose fury not dissembled speaks his griefs.
10   Then, at my suit, look graciously on him;
      Lose not so noble a friend on vain suppose,
      Nor with sour looks afflict his gentle heart.
      [*Aside to Saturninus.*]
      My lord, be rul'd by me; be won at last.
15   Dissemble all your griefs and discontents.
      You are but newly planted in your throne;
      Lest, then, the people, and patricians too,
      Upon a just survey take Titus' part,
      And so supplant you for ingratitude,
20   Which Rome reputes to be a heinous sin,
      Yield at entreats; and then let me alone.
      I'll find a day to massacre them all
      And raze their faction and their family,
      The cruel father and his traitorous sons
25   To whom I sued for my dear son's life,
      And make them know what 'tis to let a queen

Kneel in the streets and beg for grace in vain.
[*Aloud.*] Come, come, sweet Emperor; come, Andronicus;
Take up this good old man, and cheer the heart
That dies in tempest of thy angry frown. 30
Titus, I am incorporate in Rome,
And must advise the Emperor for his good.
This day all quarrels die, Andronicus.
And let it be mine honor, good my lord,
That I have reconcil'd your friends and you. 35

2 Were gracious found favor, was acceptable **3 indifferently** impartially **5 forfend** forbid **6 author** an agent **7 undertake** vouch **9 dissembled** disguised **his** to his **11 vain suppose** false or idle supposition **12 gentle** noble **14 at last** in the end **18 just survey** fair assessment (of the situation) **21 at entreats** to entreaty **let me alone** leave the rest to me **23 raze** obliterate **29 Take up** lift from kneeling (Just prior to Tamora's speech, Titus knelt before her and Saturninus.) **31 incorporate in** a part of, united with

(2)   TAMORA   [II.III.91]

SCENE: A forest near Rome

{When moments earlier Bassianus and Lavinia began cracking wise about Tamora's love life, the Queen of the Goths was anything but amused. Now, with the arrival of her sons, Chiron and Demetrius, on the scene, Tamora suddenly has the upper hand, and bites back by contriving a tale of slander and abduction.}

Have I not reason, think you, to look pale? 1
These two have 'ticed me hither to this place.
A barren detested vale you see it is;
The trees, though summer, yet forlorn and lean,
Overcome with moss and baleful mistletoe; 5
Here never shines the sun; here nothing breeds,
Unless the nightly owl or fatal raven.
And when they show'd me this abhorred pit,
They told me, here, at dead time of night,
A thousand fiends, a thousand hissing snakes, 10
Ten thousand swelling toads, as many urchins,
Would make such fearful and confused cries
As any mortal body hearing it
Should straight fall mad, or else die suddenly.

15 No sooner had they told this hellish tale,
    But straight they told me they would bind me here
    Unto the body of a dismal yew,
    And leave me to this miserable death.
    And then they call'd me foul adulteress,
20 Lascivious Goth, and all the bitterest terms
    That ever ear did hear to such effect;
    And had you not by wondrous fortune come,
    This vengeance on me had they executed.
    Revenge it, as you love your mother's life,
25 Or be ye not henceforth call'd my children.

1 look pale (Perhaps Chiron and Demetrius have mistook Tamora's
anger for illness; they've just asked her why she looks "so pale and wan.")
2 These two i.e., Bassianus and Lavinia **'ticed** enticed   **4 yet** still
5 Overcome overgrown   **7 nightly** nocturnal   **fatal** menacing, ominous
8 abhorred abominable   **11 urchins** hedgehogs (It was thought that
goblins sometimes assumed the form of a hedgehog.)   **12 fearful** dreadful
14 straight straightaway, at once   **17 body** trunk

ALTERNATES
Lavinia   [II.iii.142–178]
Tamora   [IV.iv.81–112]

TROILUS AND CRESSIDA

With the Trojan War raging in the background, Troilus and Cressida have managed to fall deeply in love with each other. Things go swimmingly between the two until Cressida is shipped over to the Grecian side as part of a prisoner exchange. Once there, Cressida quickly proves unfaithful to Troilus by taking up with a Greek commander named Diomedes.

Upon learning of Cressida's infidelity, an irate and embittered Troilus exacts his revenge on the Greeks by wreaking considerable havoc on the battlefield. But it would appear that Troilus's heroics may be all for naught, as the story ends with his beloved Troy teetering on the brink of defeat.

HELEN, wife to the King of Sparta
CRESSIDA, a Trojan maiden

PRIAM, King of Troy
TROILUS, son to Priam
PANDARUS, uncle to Cressida
DIOMEDES, a Greek commander

(1)   **CRESSIDA**   [III.II.113]

SCENE: Pandarus's orchard

{Though Cressida remains unsure how best to proceed, she can withhold her secret no longer. For better or for worse, the time has come to tell Troilus how she feels about him.}

1	Boldness comes to me now, and brings me heart.
	Prince Troilus, I have lov'd you night and day
	For many weary months. I was won, my lord,
	With the first glance that ever—pardon me;
5	If I confess much, you will play the tyrant.
	I love you now, but till now not so much
	But I might master it. In faith, I lie;
	My thoughts were like unbridled children, grown
	Too headstrong for their mother. See, we fools!
10	Why have I blabb'd? Who shall be true to us,
	When we are so unsecret to ourselves?
	But, though I lov'd you well, I woo'd you not;
	And yet, good faith, I wish'd myself a man,
	Or that we women had men's privilege
15	Of speaking first. Sweet, bid me hold my tongue,
	For in this rapture I shall surely speak
	The thing I shall repent. See, see, your silence,
	Cunning in dumbness, from my weakness draws
	My very soul of counsel! Stop my mouth.
20	My lord, I do beseech you, pardon me.
	I am asham'd. O heavens, what have I done?
	Where is my wit? I know not what I speak.
	Yet if I be false, or swerve a hair from truth,
	When time is old and hath forgot itself,
25	When waterdrops have worn the stones of Troy,
	And blind oblivion swallow'd cities up,
	And mighty states characterless are grated
	To dusty nothing, yet let memory,
	From false to false, among false maids in love,
30	Upbraid my falsehood! When th' have said "as false
	As air, as water, wind, or sandy earth,
	As fox to lamb, or wolf to heifer's calf,
	Pard to the hind, or step-dame to her son,"
	Yea, let them say, to stick the heart of falsehood,
35	"As false as Cressid."

7 But but that   **In faith** in fact, the truth is   **18 dumbness** silence
19 soul of counsel innermost thoughts and feelings   **22 wit** sound
judgment, intelligence   **26 blind** dark   **27 characterless** leaving no trace
of their existence behind them   **33 Pard** leopard   **step-dame** stepmother
34 stick stab, pierce

ALTERNATE

Cressida   [I.ii.282–295]

TWELFTH NIGHT

After being shipwrecked on the coast of Illyria, Viola adopts the guise of a young man named Cesario, and finds employment as a page to Duke Orsino. Since the Duke has made no headway of late in his attempts to woo the rich widow Olivia, he instructs Cesario to act as emissary between himself and the lady. Unfortunately, because Cesario does such a bang-up job of arguing Orsino's cause, Olivia falls for the messenger instead of the message. What's more, Olivia's beloved Cesario finds he/she has fallen in love with the Duke.

Further complicating matters is the sudden appearance in town of Viola's twin brother Sebastian, who was assumed to have been lost at sea.

Predictably enough, mistaken identities and misplaced affections soon become the order of the day. Though confusion reigns for a time, things eventually sort themselves out: Sebastian marries Olivia, while Viola drops her disguise and professes her love for her husband-to-be, the Duke.

At the same time all of the above is unfolding, Olivia's gentlewoman Maria is spearheading a plot to exact revenge on Olivia's tiresome and fussy steward, Malvolio. Their conspiracy pays off with Malvolio's imprisonment as a madman—a fate from which he is rescued only when Olivia discovers Maria & company's scheme.

OLIVIA, a rich countess
VIOLA, servant to Duke Orsino
MARIA, Olivia's gentlewoman

ORSINO, Duke of Illyria
SEBASTIAN, brother to Viola
SIR TOBY BELCH, uncle to Olivia
SIR ANDREW AGUECHEEK, companion to Sir Toby
MALVOLIO, steward to Olivia
FESTE, a jester, servant to Olivia

(1)   VIOLA   [II.ii.17]

SCENE: A street in Illyria

{Moments after leaving Olivia's house, Viola (in disguise as a boy named Cesario)
was overtaken by Olivia's steward, Malvolio. After doing his mistress's bidding—
namely, to return a ring to Cesario—Malvolio made an abrupt exit. With ring
in hand, a perplexed Viola takes a moment alone to try and sort things through.}

I left no ring with her. What mean's this lady?	1
Fortune forbid my outside have not charm'd her!	
She made good view of me; indeed, so much	
That sure methought her eyes had lost her tongue,	
For she did speak in starts distractedly.	5
She loves me, sure! The cunning of her passion	
Invites me in this churlish messenger.	
None of my lord's ring? Why, he sent her none.	
I am the man. If it be so, as 'tis,	
Poor lady, she were better love a dream.	10
Disguise, I see, thou art a wickedness	
Wherein the pregnant enemy does much.	
How easy it is for the proper-false	
In women's waxen hearts to set their forms!	
Alas, our frailty is the cause, not we,	15
For such as we are made of, such we be.	
How will this fadge? My master loves her dearly;	
And I, poor monster, fond as much on him;	
And she, mistaken, seems to dote on me.	
What will become of this? As I am man,	20
My state is desperate for my master's love;	
As I am woman—now alas the day!—	
What thriftless sighs shall poor Olivia breathe!	
O time, thou must untangle this, not I;	
It is too hard a knot for me t' untie.	25

4 lost caused her to lose   **7 Invites** lures   **in** through   **messenger** (i.e.,
Malvolio)   **8 None...ring?** (Olivia's pretense for sending Malvolio was to
return Orsino's ring, supposedly given to her by "Cesario" in the first place.)
9 the man (who Olivia desires)   **12 pregnant** resourceful
13 proper-false handsome but deceitful (men)   **14 waxen** impressionable
set their forms leave their marks   **16 such...of** i.e., feminine frailty
17 fadge end up, work out   **18 monster** strange creature (in that she is, in
a way, both man and woman)   **fond** dote   **23 thriftless** fruitless

(2)   MARIA   [II.III.131]

SCENE: Olivia's house

{In the midst of reveling with Sir Toby and the boys, Maria cooks up a plot to get even with Malvolio for all the bother he's caused them.}

1   Sweet Sir Toby, be patient for tonight. Since the youth of the Count's was today with my lady, she is much out of quiet. For Monsieur Malvolio, let me alone with him. If I do not gull him into a nayword, and make him a common recreation, do not think I have wit enough to lie straight in my bed. I know
5   I can do it. [He is] an affection'd ass, that cons state without book and utters it by great swarths; the best persuaded of himself, so cramm'd, as he thinks, with excellencies, that it is his grounds of faith that all that look on him love him; and on that vice in him will my revenge find notable cause to work. I will drop in his way some obscure epistles of love, wherein, by the color of his
10   beard, the shape of his leg, the manner of his gait, the expressure of his eye, forehead, and complexion, he shall find himself most feelingly personated. I can write very like my lady your niece; on a forgotten matter we can hardly make distinction of our hands. He shall think, by the letters that I will drop, that they come from my [lady] and that she's in love with him. O, 'twill be sport royal, I
15   warrant you. I know my physic will work with him. I will plant you two, and let the fool make a third, where he shall find the letter. Observe his construction of it. For this night, to bed, and dream on the event. Farewell.

2 out of quiet on edge, uneasy   **3 gull** trick   **nayword** proverb
3–4 common recreation general laughingstock   **5 affection'd** affected
cons ... book memorizes the phrases and mannerisms of the privileged
6 swarths heaps   **best persuaded** most fond   **10 expressure** expressive
quality   **11 feelingly personated** precisely described   **13 hands**
handwriting   **15 physic** medicine   **15–16 you ... third** (Sir Andrew,
Sir Toby, and the clown Feste, respectively)   **16 construction** interpretation

ALTERNATE
Olivia   [I.v.257–311]

THE TWO GENTLEMEN OF VERONA

Valentine and Proteus arrive at the court of the Duke of Milan intending to acquire a bit of worldly experience. In almost no time both gentlemen of Verona fall in love with the Duke's daughter, Silvia. Silvia takes a shine to Valentine as well, so she and Valentine make plans to run away together. But their plans fall apart when the Duke hears from Proteus of his daughter's intentions, and promptly banishes Valentine.

Proteus's subsequent attempt to win Silvia for himself is a dismal failure. Silvia rebuffs his advances and sets off for the woods in search of her beloved Valentine.

Meanwhile Julia, Proteus's girlfriend back in Verona, has decided to adopt the guise of a page and pursue Proteus to Milan. Once there, Julia discovers her beau's infatuation with Silvia. Undeterred (and still in disguise), Julia then joins Proteus as he seeks out Silvia—a mission that culminates in Proteus rescuing Silvia from a band of outlaws.

Things begin to settle a bit when Valentine appears on the scene and Julia reveals her true identity. Eventually, Proteus realizes that it is Julia he truly loves, and Valentine is granted Silvia's hand in marriage.

Appearing from time to time as a playful adjunct to the main story are Proteus's servant, Launce, and his indelicate dog, Crab.

JULIA, a lady of Verona, beloved of Proteus
SILVIA, daughter to the Duke of Milan, beloved of Valentine
LUCETTA, a young woman attending on Julia

DUKE OF MILAN
VALENTINE, a gentleman of Verona
PROTEUS, a gentleman of Verona
LAUNCE, servant to Proteus

(1)   JULIA   [I.ii.41]

SCENE: The garden of Julia's house

{Julia's waiting-woman, Lucetta, has entered bearing a letter from Julia's beau, Proteus. But rather than simply accept the missive (which Julia desperately wishes to do), the flighty maid opts instead for an inspired show of indignation.}

1   Now, by my modesty, a goodly broker!
        Dare you presume to harbor wanton lines?
        To whisper and conspire against my youth?
        Now, trust me, 'tis an office of great worth,
5   And you an officer fit for the place.
        There, take the paper. See it be return'd.
        Or else return no more into my sight.
        [*She gives the letter back. Lucetta Exits.*]
        And yet I would I had o'erlook'd the letter.
10   It were a shame to call her back again
        And pray her to a fault for which I chid her.
        What 'fool is she, that knows I am a maid,
        And would not force the letter to my view!
        Since maids, in modesty, say "no" to that
15   Which they would have the profferer construe "ay."
        Fie, fie, how wayward is the foolish love
        That, like a testy babe, will scratch the nurse
        And presently, all humbled, kiss the rod!
        How churlishly I chid Lucetta hence,
20   When willingly I would have had her here!
        How angerly I taught my brow to frown,
        When inward joy enforc'd my heart to smile!
        My penance is to call Lucetta back
        And ask remission for my folly past.
25   What ho! Lucetta!

     1 broker agent, go-between   **5 place** position   **9 would** wish   **o'er'look'd**
     read over   **11 pray** entreat   **to a fault** to commit a fault, to do something
     wrong   **chid** scolded, chided   **12 'fool** a fool   **15 construe** interpret as
     16 Fie (an expression of disgust)   **18 presently** immediately afterward,
     instantly   **rod** stick or switch (used to punish the "testy babe")   **19 hence**
     away   **21 angerly** angrily   **22 enforc'd** urged   **24 remission** forgiveness

(2)   JULIA   [I.ii.102]

SCENE: The garden of Julia's house

{When, moments earlier, Julia was presented a letter from her beloved Proteus, she put on a most convincing show of irritation, ripping up the note into little pieces. But now that she is alone, the lady's true sentiments emerge, as she scurries about to collect the fragments of her lover's missive.}

O hateful hands, to tear such loving words!   1
Injurious wasps, to feed on such sweet honey
And kill the bees that yield it with your stings!
I'll kiss each several paper for amends.
Look, here is writ "kind Julia." Unkind Julia!   5
As in revenge of thy ingratitude,
I throw thy name against the bruising stones,
Trampling contemptuously on thy disdain.
And here is writ "love-wounded Proteus."
Poor Wounded name! My bosom as a bed   10
Shall lodge thee till thy wound be throughly heal'd;
And thus I search it with a sovereign kiss.
But twice or thrice was "Proteus" written down.
Be calm, good wind, blow not a word away
Till I have found each letter in the letter,   15
Except mine own name; that, some whirlwind bear
Unto a ragged, fearful, hanging rock,
And throw it thence into the raging sea!
Lo, here in one line is his name twice writ,
"Poor forlorn Proteus, passionate Proteus,   20
To the sweet Julia"—that I'll tear away—
And yet I will not, sith so prettily
He couples it to his complaining names.
Thus will I fold them one upon another.
Now kiss, embrace, contend, do what you will.   25

2 wasps (referring to her fingers)   **4 several** separate (scrap of)
11 throughly thoroughly   **12 search** probe, cleanse (as one would with an actual wound)   **sovereign** healing   **17 fearful** terrible, frightening   **hanging rock** cliff   **21 that** i.e., the mention of her name   **22 sith** since
23 complaining lamenting   **25 contend** fight

(3)   JULIA   [IV.IV.183]

SCENE: Outside the Duke of Milan's palace

{Moments ago, Silvia left a portrait of herself with Julia, which Julia is now
supposed to pass on to Proteus. Before she does so, however, Julia takes a moment
to try and ascertain exactly what it is (in Proteus's opinion, anyway) Silvia's got
that she doesn't.}

1   Alas, how love can trifle with itself!
     Here is her picture. Let me see; I think
     If I had such a tire, this face of mine
     Were full as lovely as is this of hers;
5   And yet the painter flatter'd her a little,
     Unless I flatter with myself too much.
     Her hair is auburn, mine is perfect yellow.
     If that be all the difference in this love,
     I'll get me such a color'd periwig.
10   Her eyes are gray as glass, and so are mine;
     Ay, but her forehead's low, and mine's as high.
     What should it be that he respects in her
     But I can make respective in myself,
     If this fond love were not a blinded god?
15   Come, shadow, come, and take this shadow up,
     For 'tis thy rival. O thou senseless form,
     Thou shalt be worship'd, kiss'd, lov'd, and ador'd;
     And were there sense in his idolatry,
     My substance should be statue in thy stead.
20   I'll use thee kindly for thy mistress' sake,
     That us'd me so; or else, by Jove I vow,
     I should have scratch'd out your unseeing eyes,
     To make my master out of love with thee!

3 tire headdress   **4 full** every bit   **9 periwig** wig   **11 as high** i.e., as high
as Silvia's is low (High foreheads were much admired in Elizabethan times.)
12 respects values, esteems   **13 respective** worthy of respect, worth
caring about   **14 fond** infatuated, foolish   **15 Come, shadow** come, mere
shadow of my true self (Julia is employing a bit of self-disparagement in hopes
of spurring herself into action.)   **take . . . up** accept the challenge which this
portrait ("shadow") presents   **16 senseless** inanimate, insensible   **18 his**
i.e., Proteus's   **19 substance** real self   **statue** (his) idol   **20 use** treat
21 us'd me so (The kind treatment to which Julia refers can be found at
IV.iv.133–178.)

THE WINTER'S TALE

For no particularly good reason, Leontes, the King of Sicilia, accuses his wife, Hermione, of stepping out on him with his friend, Polixenes. Though Polixenes manages to escape the wrath of Leontes by returning to his home in Bohemia, Hermione is not so fortunate.

Shortly after being thrown in prison by her husband, Hermione gives birth to a daughter, who Leontes declares is "a bastard by Polixenes," and so orders it abandoned in some remote place. Although Hermione is cleared at her trial of any wrongdoing, it's only when word arrives that she has suddenly taken ill and died that a repentant Leontes finally sees the error of his ways.

Hermione's babe, meanwhile, is abandoned on the coast of Bohemia. But fortunately, the tot is soon discovered by a kindly shepherd, who proceeds to raise her as his own daughter, Perdita.

At the age of sixteen, Perdita falls in love with Florizel, the son of Polixenes. Since Polixenes deems a poor shepherd's daughter unworthy of his son, he thwarts their plans for marriage. The two lovers thus sail off to Sicilia, where Leontes soon figures out that Perdita is his long-lost daughter. Eventually, Polixenes and Leontes are reconciled, and arrangements are made for the marriage of Florizel and Perdita. Adding to the happy proceedings is a surprise appearance by Hermione; evidently, news of the Queen's death was greatly exaggerated.

HERMIONE, queen to Leontes
PERDITA, daughter to Leontes and Hermione
PAULINA, wife to Antigonus

LEONTES, King of Sicilia
ANTIGONUS, a lord of Sicilia
POLIXENES, King of Bohemia
FLORIZEL, son to Polixenes
SHEPHERD, guardian to Perdita
CLOWN, son to the shepherd
AUTOLYCUS, a rogue

(1)   HERMIONE   [III.ii.22]

SCENE: A court of justice in Sicilia

{For no apparent reason, Leontes has accused Hermione of cheating on him with the King of Bohemia. Since Hermione's day in court has arrived, she now stands before her husband and others to speak on her own behalf.}

1	Since what I am to say must be but that
	Which contradicts my accusation, and
	The testimony on my part no other
	But what comes from myself, it shall scarce boot me
5	To say "Not guilty." Mine integrity,
	Being counted falsehood, shall, as I express it,
	Be so receiv'd. But thus: if pow'rs divine
	Behold our human actions, as they do,
	I doubt not then but innocence shall make
10	False accusation blush, and tyranny
	Tremble at patience. You, my lord, best know,
	Who least will seem to do so, my past life
	Hath been as continent, as chaste, as true,
	As I am now unhappy; which is more
15	Than history can pattern, though devis'd
	And play'd to take spectators. For behold me—
	A fellow of the royal bed, which owe
	A moi'ty of the throne, a great king's daughter,
	The mother to a hopeful prince—here standing
20	To prate and talk for life and honor 'fore
	Who please to come and hear. For life, I prize it
	As I weigh grief, which I would spare. For honor,
	'Tis a derivative from me to mine,
	And only that I stand for. I appeal
25	To your own conscience, sir, before Polixenes
	Came to your court, how I was in your grace,
	How merited to be so; since he came,
	With what encounter so uncurrent I
	Have strain'd t' appear thus; if one jot beyond
30	The bound of honor, or in act or will
	That way inclining, hard'ned be the hearts
	Of all that hear me, and my near'st of kin
	Cry fie upon my grave! More than mistress of
	Which comes to me in name of fault, I must not
35	At all acknowledge. For Polixenes,
	With whom I am accus'd, I do confess

I lov'd him as in honor he requir'd;
With such a kind of love as might become
A lady like me; with a love even such,
So and no other, as yourself commanded;   40
Which not to have done I think had been in me
Both disobedience and ingratitude
To you and toward your friend, whose love had spoke,
Even since it could speak, from an infant, freely
That it was yours. Now, for conspiracy,   45
I know not how it tastes, though it be dish'd
For me to try how. Sir, my life stands in
The level of your dreams, which I'll lay down.

4 boot serve, profit   **12 seem ... so** appear as though you do (know)
14 which (an unhappiness) which   **15 Than ... pattern** than any story or
drama can match   **16 take** please, charm   **17 fellow** companion   **which
owe** who owns   **18 moi'ty** share, half   **19 hopeful prince** heir apparent
20 prate babble   **22 which ... spare** and would as readily give it up
23 'Tis ... mine it is something that is passed on from me to my
descendants   **24 stand for** defend, stand up for   **25 conscience** internal
conviction, judgment   **28–29 With ... thus** with what sort of unacceptable
behavior, I have exceeded all limits of propriety, and thus appear in this way
(disgraced and on trial)   **33 fie** (an exclamation of disgust)   **mistress**
possessor   **34 Which** that which   **fault** common human frailty
37 requir'd merited   **45 for** as for   **46 dish'd** served up, offered   **48 level**
aim   **dreams** delusions, fantasies

(2)   HERMIONE   [III.ii.91]

SCENE: A court of justice in Sicilia

*{Leontes, unmoved by Hermione's testimony (see preceding entry), has threatened
her with torture and death. Much to her credit, Hermione will not be cowed.}*

Sir, spare your threats.   1
The bug which you would fright me with I seek.
To me can life be no commodity.
The crown and comfort of my life, your favor,
I do give lost; for I do feel it gone,   5
But know not how it went. My second joy
And first-fruits of my body, from his presence

I am barr'd, like one infectious. My third comfort,
Starr'd most unluckily, is from my breast,
10   The innocent milk in it most innocent mouth,
Hal'd out to murder; myself on every post
Proclaim'd a strumpet; with immodest hatred
The child-bed privilege denied, which 'longs
To women of all fashion; lastly, hurried
15   Here to this place, i' th' open air, before
I have got strength of limit. Now, my liege,
Tell me what blessings I have here alive,
That I should fear to die? Therefore proceed.
But yet hear this; mistake me not. No life,
20   I prize it not a straw; but for mine honor,
Which I would free, if I shall be condemn'd
Upon surmises, all proofs sleeping else
But what your jealousies awake, I tell you
'Tis rigor and not law. Your honors all,
25   I do refer me to the oracle.
Apollo be my judge!

2 bug bogeyman, hobgoblin (or other such imaginary object of terror)
3 no commodity of no use or valor   **5 give** concede as, account
7 first-fruits first-born   **9 Starr'd most unluckily** born under unlucky
stars   **10 it** its   **11 Hal'd** hauled   **post** (Public notices announcing legal
actions like the one against Hermione were commonly attached to posts.)
12 immodest immoderate   **13 child-bed privilege** privilege of
recuperating in seclusion after giving birth   **'longs** belongs   **14 all fashion**
every rank or social status   **16 got...limit** regained my strength (after
childbirth)   **19 mistake me not** do not misunderstand me   **No life** i.e.,
I do not beg for life   **21 free** clear, absolve   **24 rigor** tyranny   **Your
honors** honorable gentlemen (referring to the nobles and court officials also
present)   **25 refer me** submit my grievance

(3)   PAULINA   [III.ii.175]

SCENE: A court of justice in Sicilia

*{As Hermione was defending herself against a false charge of marital infidelity
(see entry (1), above), word arrived that her young son had suddenly died.
The Queen fainted and was taken from the courtroom. A few moments later,
Paulina enters the court in near hysteria as the bearer of bad tidings.}*

What studied torments, tyrant, hast for me? 1
What wheels? Racks? Fires? What flaying? Boiling
In leads or oils? What old or newer torture
Must I receive, whose every word deserves
To taste of thy most worst? Thy tyranny, 5
Together working with thy jealousies—
Fancies too weak for boys, too green and idle
For girls of nine—O, think what they have done,
And then run mad indeed, stark mad! For all
Thy by-gone fooleries were but spices of it. 10
That thou betray'dst Polixenes, 'twas nothing;
That did but show thee of a fool, inconstant
And damnable ingrateful. Nor was 't much
That would'st have poison'd good Camillo's honor,
To have him kill a king—poor trespasses, 15
More monstrous standing by; whereof I reckon
The casting forth to crows thy baby-daughter
To be or none or little, though a devil
Would have shed water out of fire ere done 't.
Nor is 't directly laid to thee, the death 20
Of the young Prince, whose honorable thoughts—
Thoughts high for one so tender—cleft the heart
That could conceive a gross and foolish sire
Blemish'd his gracious dam. This is not, no,
Laid to thy answer. But the last—O lords, 25
When I have said, cry "Woe!"—the Queen, the Queen,
The sweet'st, dear'st creature's dead, and vengeance for 't
Not dropp'd down yet. Go and see. If you can bring
Tincture or luster in her lip, her eye,
Heat outwardly or breath within, I'll serve you 30
As I would do the gods. But, O thou tyrant!
Do not repent these things, for they are heavier
Than all thy woes can stir. Therefore betake thee
To nothing but despair. A thousand knees,
Ten thousand years together, naked, fasting, 35
Upon a barren mountain, and still winter
In storm perpetual, could not move the gods
To look that way thou wert.

1 studied rehearsed, carefully prepared **tyrant** (Paulina is addressing
Leontes.) **hast** have you **2 wheels, racks** (common instruments of
torture, dating from the Middle Ages) **7 Fancies** imaginings (that are)
10 fooleries acts of folly **spices** samples, tastes **15 poor** petty, trivial
16 More . . . by when even more hideous sins stand near them for

comparison   **19 shed ... fire** wept in hell   **20 laid to** accused of
22 tender young   **23 a** that a   **sire** father   **24 dam** mother
25 Laid ... answer an accusation to which you need answer   **26 said** i.e.,
said what I am about to say   **28 not ... yet** has not yet descended   **33 woe
can stir** sorrow and penance can atone for   **36 still** always

ALTERNATES
Hermione   [II.i.105–124]
Perdita   [IV.iv.71–135]

GUIDE TO PRONUNCIATION

Everything's going like clockwork. The pace feels right, you're focused, and your points are being made. This Shakespeare thing is a snap. And then, just like that—something's wrong. Those same people at the table in front of you, who seconds earlier were hanging on every word of your monologue, now seem distracted. They're still listening—sort of—but their attention has been broken in two. What on earth could have happened?

In truth, almost anything. But when it comes to performing Shakespeare, an all-too-common culprit in this kind of disruption is faulty pronunciation. Perhaps nothing derails a smooth-running monologue quite so quickly as a botched moniker.

The bad news is that this sort of thing happens all the time. The good news is that it's entirely preventable. All you need is the resolve to get it right and a resource to help you do just that. The first part of the equation is your responsibility; the second is taken care of with this appendix.

The essentials of this pronunciation guide are as follows:

* Syllables are separated by a hyphen.
* Accented syllables are CAPITALIZED.
* Syllables or parts of syllables that are *italicized* indicate vowel sounds that are lightly articulated. For example, the sound of <*uh*> is identical to that of <uh>, but it's uttered for a shorter length of time: an eighth note versus a quarter, if you will.

In an attempt to strike a happy medium between ease of use and precision, a phonetic-based key to pronunciation has been adopted. The guide's basic sounds are as follows:

Vowel Sounds

A

A, a . . . as in MAN, ASK, FLAP
AH, ah . . . as in DOT, ODD, JOG
AHR, ahr . . . as in CAR, FAR, MARK
AIR, air . . . as in CARE, WEAR, FAIR

AY, ay . . . as in DAY, WEIGHT, THEY
AW, aw . . . as in RAW, BALL, TALK

E

E, e . . . as in PET, LESS, WRECK
EE, ee . . . as in EAT, WE, DEED

EER, eer . . . as in JEER, NEAR,
PIER

I

I, i . . . as in TRIP, SIT, PIN

Y, y . . . as in ICE, TRY, NIGHT

O

OH, oh . . . as in TOE, DOUGH,
OLD
OO, oo . . . as in OOZE, TWO,
SOUP
OR, or . . . as in FOR, WAR,
MORE

OOR, oor . . . as in TOUR,
LURE
OW, ow . . . as in HOW, POUT,
DOWN
OY, oy . . . as in TOY, OIL,
COIN

U

UH, uh . . . as in DUMB, SON, UP
UR, ur . . . as in SPUR, STIR, EARN

UU, uu . . . as in HOOD, PULL,
TOOK

Consonant Sounds

B, b . . . as in BOB, CRAB
CH, ch . . . as in CHOP,
DUTCH
D, d . . . as in DID, POD
F, f . . . as in FLUFF, LAUGH
G, g . . . as in GAG, RUG
H, h . . . as in HOT, HIP
J, j . . . as in JUICE, CAGE
K, k . . . as in CAKE, COOK
L, l . . . as in LULL, ALE
M, m . . . as in MOM, SOME
N, n . . . as in NUN, SOON

NG, ng . . . as in RING, BANG
P, p . . . as in POP, MAP
R, r . . . as in RIP, MORE
S, s . . . as in SASS, SIP
T, t . . . as in TOT, CAST
TH, th . . . as in PATH,
THOUGHT
V, v . . . as in VERY, HIVE
W, w . . . as in WOW, QUIT
Y, y . . . as in YES, YAWN
Z, z . . . as in HAZE, ZOO
ZH, zh . . . as in BEIGE

Listed below are the most widely accepted pronunciations of character and location names appearing in *Shakespeare for One*. Commonly recognized words like *Henry* and *Verona* have been omitted, since most who use this book will know them already. For those who don't, any standard dictionary can fill in the gaps.

ACHERON	(AK-*uh*-rahn)
ACTAEON	(ak-TEE-*uh*n)
ADRIANA	(ay-dree-AH-n*uh*)
AENEAS	(ee-NEE-*uh*s)
AEOLUS	(EE-*oh*-luhs)
AGAMEMNON	(ag-*uh*-MEM-nahn)
AGINCOURT	(AJ-in-kort)
AGUECHEEK	(AY-gyoo-cheek)
ALBANY	(AWL-b*uh*-nee)
ALBION	(AL-bee-ahn)
ALCIBIADES	(al-si-BY-*uh*-deez)
AMIAMON	(*uh*-MY-mahn)
AMIENS	(AY-mi-enz)
ANCHISES	(an-KY-seez)
ANDRONICUS, MARCUS	(MAR-kuhs an-DRON-i-kuhs)
ANDRONICUS, TITUS	(TY-tuhs an-DRON-i-kuhs)
ANGIERS	(AN-jeerz)
ANJOU	(AN-joo)
ANTENOR	(an-TEE-nur)
ANTHROPOPHAGI	(an-throh-PAHF-*uh*-jy)
ANTIGONUS	(an-TIG-*oh*-nuhs)
ANTIOCHUS	(an-TY-*oh*-kuhs)
ANTIPHOLUS	(an-TIF-oh-luhs)
ANTIPODES	(an-TIP-*oh*-deez)
ANTONY	(AN-t*oh*-nee)
APEMANTUS	(ap-e-MAN-tuhs)
ARGUS	(AHR-guhs)
ARIEL	(E-ree-*e*l or AIR-*ee*-el)
ARMADO	(ahr-MAH-doh)
ARRAGON	(AR-*uh*-gahn)
ASCANIUS	(as-KAY-n*ee*-uhs)
ATE	(AY-tee)
AUTOLYCUS	(aw-TAHL-i-kuhs)
BACCHUS	(BAK-*uh*s)
BALTHAZAR	(bal-tha-ZAHR or bal-TAH-zahr)
BANQUO	(BAN-kwoh)
BAPTISTA	(bap-TEES-t*ah*)
BARBASON	(BAHR-b*uh*-suhn)
BARDOLPH	(BAHR-dawlf)
BASIMECU	(baz-i-m*uh*-KOO)
BASSANIO	(ba-SAH-nee-oh)

BEATRICE	(BEE-*uh*-tris)
BEAUFORT	(BOH-furt)
BELARIUS	(bel-AH-ree-uhs or be-LAY-ree-uhs)
BELLARIO	(be-LAH-ree-oh)
BENVOLIO	(ben-VOH-*lee*-oh)
BEROWNE	(be-ROON)
BERTRAM	(BUR-tr*uh*m)
BLANCHE	(BLAHNSH)
BOHEMIA	(boh-HEE-mee-*uh*)
BOLINGBROKE	(BO-ling-bruuk)
BOYET	(boy-ET)
BRABANTIO	(bra-BAN-shoh)
BRITAINE	(bre-TAN-y*uh*)
BURGUNDY	(BUR-guhn-dee)
BURY ST. EDMUNDS	(BE-ree SAYNT ED-muhndz)
CAESAR, JULIUS	(JOOL-yuhs SEE-zur)
CAIUS MARCIUS	(KAY-uhs or KAY-yuhs MAHR-shuhs)
CALAIS	(ka-LAY)
CALIBAN	(KAL-i-ban)
CALPURNIA	(kal-PUR-n*ee*-*uh*)
CAMILLO	(ka-MIL-oh)
CAMPEIUS	(kam-PAY-uhs)
CAPULET	(KAP-yoo-let)
CARLISLE	(kahr-LYL)
CASCA	(KAS-k*uh*)
CASSIO	(KAS-ee-oh)
CASSIUS	(KAS-ee-uhs)
CATO	(KAY-toh)
CAWDOR	(KAW-dur)
CERBERUS	(SUR-be-ruhs)
CERIMON	(SER-i-mahn)
CESARIO	(se-ZAH-ree-oh)
CHAM	(KAM)
CHARMIAN	(CHAHR-mee-*uh*n)
CHIRON	(KY-rahn)
CICERO	(SIS-*uh*-roh)
CLEON	(KLEE-ahn)
CLOTEN	(KLOH-t*uh*n)
COLBRAND	(KOHL-brand)
COLOSSUS	(k*o*-LAHS-*uh*s)

COMINIUS	(kah-MIN-ee-uhs)
CORDELIA	(kor-DEE-lyuh)
CORIOLANUS	(kor-ee-oh-LAY-nuhs)
CRAB	(KRAB)
CRESSIDA	(KRES-i-d*uh*)
CRISPIAN	(KRIS-pee-*a*n)
CRISPIN	(KRIS-pin)
CROMER	(KROH-mur)
CYMBELINE	(SIM-be-leen)
CYTHEREA	(sith-e-REE-*uh*)
DE BURGH	(D *UH* BURG)
DE LA POLE	(DE LAH POOL)
DEMETRIUS	(d*ee*-MEE-tri-uhs)
DESDEMONA	(dez-de-MOH-n*uh*)
DEUCALION	(dyoo-KAY-lee-*uh*n)
DIAN	(DY-an)
DIONYZA	(dy-oh-NY-z*uh*)
DORSET	(DOR-set)
DROMIO	(DROH-mee-oh)
DUMAINE	(dyoo-MAYN)
ELSINORE	(EL-si-nohr)
ENOBARBUS	(ee-noh-BAHR-buhs)
EPHESUS	(EF-e-suhs)
EROS	(EE-rahs)
EXETER	(EKS-*uh*-tur)
FALCONBRIDGE	(FAWL-k*uh*n-brij or FAW-k*uh*n-brij)
FALSTAFF	(FAWL-staf)
FENTON	(FEN-t*uh*n)
FLORIZEL	(FLAHR-i-zel)
FORTINBRAS	(FOR-tin-brahs)
FULVIA	(FUHL-vee-*uh*)
GADSHILL	(GADZ-hil)
GAUNT	(GAHNT)
GIS	(JIS)
GLAMIS	(GLAHM-is)
GLOUCESTER	(GLAHS-tur)

GLOUCESTERSHIRE	(GLAHS-tur-shir)
GONERIL	(GAHN-*uh*-ril)
GRATIANO	(grah-shee-AH-noh)
GRUMIO	(GROO-mee-oh or GROO-meeoh)
HARFLEUR	(HAHR-flur)
HECATE	(HEK-*uh*t or HEK-*uh*-tee)
HECUBA	(HEK-yoo-b*uh*)
HELENUS	(HEL-e-nuhs)
HEREFORD	(HUR-f*u*rd)
HERMIA	(HUR-mee-*uh*)
HERMIONE	(hur-MY-*oh*-n*ee*)
HERNE	(HURN)
HERO	(HE-roh)
HESPERIDES	(hes-PER-i-deez)
HESPERUS	(HES-p*uh*-ruhs)
HOLOFERNES	(hahl-*oh*-FUR-neez)
HORATIO	(hoh-RAY-shoh)
HOTSPUR	(HAHT-spur)
HYPERION	(hy-PEER-ee-*uh*n)
HYRCANIA	(hur-KAY-nee-*uh*)
IACHIMO	(EEAH-k*i*-moh or EEAH-kee-moh)
IAGO	(EEAH-goh)
IMOGEN	(IM-oh-jen)
IRAS	(EYE-rahs)
ISABELLA	(iz-*uh*-BEL-*uh*)
JAQUENETTA	(jak-*e*-NET-*uh*)
JAQUES	(JAY-kweez)
JULIA	(JYOOL-i-*uh*)
JULIET	(JYOOL-yet or JYOO-lee-et)
KATHARINA	(kat-*uh*-REE-n*uh*)
LA PUCELLE	(LAH puu-SEL)
LAERTES	(lay-UR-teez)
LAUNCE	(LAHNS or LAWNS)
LAUNCELOT GOBBO	(LAHN-s*e*-laht GAHB-boh)
LAVINIA	(l*uh*-VIN-ee-*uh*)
LE BON	(LE BAHN)

LEDA	(LEE-d*uh*)
LEONATO	(lee-oh-NAH-toh)
	(or lay-oh-NAH-toh)
LEONINE	(LEE-*oh*-nyn)
LEONTES	(lee-AHN-teez)
LICHAS	(LY-kas)
LONGAVILLE	(LAHNG-g*uh*-vil)
LUCENTIO	(loo-CHEN-seeoh)
LUCIANA	(loo-shee-AH-n*uh*)
LUCIUS	(LOO-shuhs)
LUCRECE	(loo-KREES or LOO-krees)
LYMOGES	(li-MOHZH)
LYSANDER	(ly-SAN-dur)
MAB	(MAB)
MACBETH	(mak-BETH)
MACDUFF	(mak-DUHF)
MACHIAVEL	(mak-ee-*uh*-VEL)
MALVOLIO	(mal-VOH-lee-oh)
MARIA [From *Love's Labor's Lost*]	(mah-REE-*uh*)
MARIA [From *Twelfth Night*]	(ma-RY-*uh*)
MARINA	(mah-REE-n*uh*)
MARULLUS	(ma-RUHL-uhs)
MENENIUS AGRIPPA	(me-NEE-nee-uhs *uh*-GRIP-*uh*)
MERCUTIO	(mer-KYOO-sheeoh)
MESSINA	(me-SEE-n*uh*)
MILAN	(mi-LAN)
MONMOUTH	(MAHN-muhth)
MONTAGUE	(MAHN-t*uh*-gyoo)
NAVARRE	(nah-VAHR)
NERISSA	(ne-RIS-*uh*)
NESSUS	(NES-uhs)
NESTOR	(NES-tur)
NIOBE	(NY-*oh*-bee)
NORTHUMBERLAND	(nor-THUHM-bur-l*uh*nd)
NYM	(NIM)
OBERON	(OH-be-rahn)
OCTAVIUS	(ahk-TAY-vee-uhs)
OPHELIA	(oh-FEEL-y*uh*)
ORLEANS	(OR-lee-*uh*nz)

OSWALD	(AHZ-w*uh*ld)
OTHELLO	(oh-THEL-oh)
PADUA	(PAD-yoo-*uh*)
PALATINE	(PAL-*uh*-tyn or PAL-*uh*-tin)
PANDARUS	(PAN-d*uh*-ruhs)
PANDULPH	(PAN-duhlf)
PARIS	(PA-ris)
PAROLLES	(pah-RAHL-es or pay-ROHL-es)
PATAY	(pah-TAY)
PAULINA	(paw-LEE-n*uh*)
PEDRO	(PAY-droh)
PERDITA	(PUR-di-t*uh*)
PERICLES	(PER-i-kleez)
PETO	(PEE-toh)
PETRUCHIO	(pe-TROOCH-eeoh or pe-TROO-keeoh)
PHAETHON	(FAY-e-th*uh*n)
PHEBE	(FEE-bee)
PHILOMEL	(FIL-*oh*-mel)
PHILOMELA	(fil-*oh*-MEE-l*uh*)
PHOEBUS	(FEE-buhs)
PISANIO	(pee-ZAH-neeoh)
PISTOL	(PIS-t*uh*l)
PLANTAGENET	(plan-TAJ-*uh*-net)
POINS	(POYNZ)
POLIXENES	(poh-LIKS-*uh*-neez)
POLONIUS	(p*oh*-LOH-nee-uhs)
POMFRET	(PAHM-fret)
POMPEY	(PAHM-pee)
PORTIA	(POR-sh*uh*)
POSTHUMUS	(PAHS-tyoo-muhs)
PRIAM	(PRY-am)
PROGNE	(PRAHG-nee)
PROSPERO	(PRAHS-pe-roh)
PROTEUS	(PROH-tee-uhs)
PYRAMUS	(PIR-*uh*-muhs)
QUINCE	(KWINS)
REGAN	(RAY-g*uh*n)
REYNALDO	(ray-NAWL-doh)

RODERIGO	(rahd-*uh*-REE-goh)
ROMEO	(ROH-meeoh)
ROSALIND	(RAHZ-*uh*-lind)
ROSALINE	(ROHZ-*uh*-lyn)
ROSSILLION	(roo-SIL-y*uh*n)
ROUEN	(roo-AHN or rohn)
RUTLAND	(RUHT-l*uh*nd)
SAINT ALBANS	(saynt AWL-b*uh*nz)
SALISBURY	(SAWLZ-b*uh*-ree)
SATURNINUS	(sat-ur-NY-nuhs)
SAXONY	(SAK-s*oh*-nee)
SEACOLE	(SEE-kohl)
SEBASTIAN	(se-BAS-ti*uh*n)
SHREWSBURY	(SHROOZ-b*uh*-ree)
SHYLOCK	(SHY-lahk)
SICILIA	(si-SIL-i-*uh*)
SICILS	(SIS-ilz)
SILVIA	(SIL-vee-*uh*)
SILVIUS	(SIL-vee-uhs)
SINON	(SY-n*ah*n)
SOMERSET	(SUHM-ur-set)
STARVELING	(STAHRV-ling)
STRACHY	(STRACH-ee or STRAHK-ee)
SUFFOLK	(SUHF-*uh*k)
TAMORA	(TAM-oh-r*uh*)
TAMWORTH	(TAM-wurth)
TARQUIN	(TAHR-kwin)
TEARSHEET	(TAIR-sheet)
TEREUS	(TEE-roos or TEE-r*ee*-uhs)
TERMAGANT	(TUR-mah-g*uh*nt)
TEWKESBURY	(TYOOKS-b*uh*-ree)
THAISA	(thay-IS-*uh* or thay-IZ-*uh*)
THARSUS	(TAHR-suhs)
THERSITES	(thur-SY-teez)
THESEUS	(THEE-see-uhs)
THISBY	(THIZ-b*ee*)
THRACIAN	(THRAY-sh*uh*n)
TIMON	(TY-m*uh*n)
TITANIA	(ti-TAHN-y*uh*)
TITINIUS	(ti-TIN-*ee*-uhs or ti-TIN-yuhs)

TRINCULO	(TRING-kyoo-loh)
TROILUS	(TROY-luhs)
TULLUS AUFIDIUS	(TUHL-uhs aw-FID-ee-uhs)
TYBALT	(TIB-*uh*lt)
TYRREL	(TIR-*e*l)
ULYSSES	(yoo-LIS-eez)
URSULA	(UR-syoo-l*uh*)
VALENTINE	(VAL-*uh*n-tyn)
VINCENTIO	(veen-CHEN-seeoh)
VIOLA	(VEE-oh-lah or VY-oh-lah)
VOLUMNIA	(voh-LUHM-nee-*uh*)
WARWICK	(WOR-ik)
WESTMINSTER	(WEST-min-stur)
WESTMORLAND	(WEST-m*ur*-l*uh*nd)
WOLSEY	(WUUL-zee)
YORICK	(YOR-ik)

THE LONG AND SHORT OF IT

Time is usually of the essence when it comes to choosing a monologue. How long the piece should be almost always depends on how it's going to be used. At one end of the spectrum lies the typical audition: most likely a lickety-split affair allowing you no more than two or three minutes in which to display your Shakespearean wares. At the other extreme is the relatively indulgent pace of the classroom, where a more thorough exploration of lengthier pieces is often the order of the day.

Of the 88 monologues presented in this volume of *Shakespeare for One,* two-thirds run between 25 and 45 lines, and thus are suitable for most applications. Should the time come, however, when only a particularly brief or extended selection will do, one the following entries will likely fill the bill.

Monologues of Fewer Than 25 Lines

ANTONY AND CLEOPATRA
- (1) Cleopatra
- (2) Cleopatra
- (3) Cleopatra

AS YOU LIKE IT
- (1) Celia
- (5) Rosalind

HENRY V
- (1) Hostess

HENRY VI, PART 1
- (1) Joan La Pucelle

JULIUS CAESAR
- (2) Calpurnia

A MIDSUMMER NIGHT'S DREAM
- (2) Helena

MACBETH
    (4) Lady Macbeth

THE MERCHANT OF VENICE
    (2) Portia

THE MERRY WIVES OF WINDSOR
    (2) Mistress Ford

OTHELLO
    (1) Emilia

RICHARD III
    (2) Lady Anne

THE TWO GENTLEMEN OF VERONA
    (1) Julia
    (3) Julia

Monologues of More Than 45 Lines

AS YOU LIKE IT
    (2) Rosalind

CORIOLANUS
    (1) Volumnia
    (2) Volumnia

HENRY IV, PART 2
    (1) Lady Percy

HENRY VI, PART 2
    (3) Margaret

HENRY VIII
    (2) Katharine

JULIUS CAESAR
    (1) Portia

MEASURE FOR MEASURE
    (1) Isabella

THE MERCHANT OF VENICE
    (1) Portia

MUCH ADO ABOUT NOTHING
    (1) Hero

ROMEO AND JULIET
    (1) Nurse
    (5) Juliet

THE WINTER'S TALE
    (1) Hermione

STRAIGHT TALK AND RHYME

Essentially, the fruit of Shakespeare's genius comes in one of three varieties: blank verse, rhyming verse, or prose. Since blank verse is used in the majority of his plays, it follows that most of the entries in *Shakespeare for One* are of the same stripe. Monologues *not* written in blank verse are singled out below.

Prose

AS YOU LIKE IT
    (2) Rosalind
    (5) Rosalind

HENRY V
    (1) Hostess

MACBETH
    (1) Lady Macbeth
    (4) Lady Macbeth

THE MERCHANT OF VENICE
    (1) Portia

THE MERRY WIVES OF WINDSOR
    (1) Mistress Page
    (2) Mistress Ford
    (3) Mistress Quickly

OTHELLO
    (2) Emilia

TWELFTH NIGHT
    (2) Maria

Rhyme

THE COMEDY OF ERRORS
  (1) Adriana
  (3) Luciana

HAMLET
  (1) Ophelia

MACBETH
  (3) Hecate

A MIDSUMMER NIGHT'S DREAM
  (1) Helena

SHAKESPEARE'S GREATEST HITS

Suggestions for the Initiates

A wide array of options is an asset in most cases. But it can sometimes leave a person feeling overwhelmed. Take, for example, the actor who's just beginning to delve into the daunting world of classical monologues. He or she faces enough challenges as it is without having to sift through dozens of speeches hoping to find one that's particularly suited to a newcomer's needs.

With that in mind, offered below is a not-to-be-taken-too-seriously collection of greatest hits from *Shakespeare for One*: a score of friendly monologues deemed especially suitable for the uncertain actor who could use a nudge in the right direction.

Among the criteria considered in drawing up this list were:

- **Freshness**. Underexposed speeches had a big leg up on the competition. All warhorses ("To be, or not to be . . . ") were left in the stable.
- **Pace**. The selection was expected to generate a sense of momentum and be active rather than primarily introspective in nature.
- **Structure**. The piece had to be relatively straightforward in form, with a minimum of obscure references and syntactic mazes.
- **Staging**. It was considered a plus if the monologue suggested interesting or amusing physical possibilities. It was the kiss of death if too many prop or business requirements threatened to be a distraction.
- ***Death scenes need not apply***.

Don't forget, the list that follows doesn't really claim to be the "best" of Shakespeare. But if you're in need of a monologue that is accessible, coherent, and hasn't already been worked to death, this Shakespearean top-twenty is a worthy place to start looking.

ALL'S WELL THAT ENDS WELL
(3) Helena

ANTONY AND CLEOPATRA
(1) Cleopatra

AS YOU LIKE IT
(3) Rosalind

AS YOU LIKE IT
(4) Phebe

CYMBELINE
(1) Imogen

HENRY VI, PART 1
(3) Joan La Pucelle

HENRY VI, PART 2
(1) Eleanor

HENRY VI, PART 3
(1) Queen Margaret

JULIUS CAESAR
(1) Portia

KING JOHN
(1) Constance

MACBETH
(2) Lady Macbeth

MEASURE FOR MEASURE
(1) Isabella

THE MERCHANT OF VENICE
(1) Portia

THE MERRY WIVES OF WINDSOR
(1) Mistress Page
(3) Mistress Quickly

OTHELLO
(2) Emilia

RICHARD III
(2) Lady Anne

ROMEO AND JULIET
   (4) Juliet

TROILUS AND CRESSIDA
   (1) Cressida

THE TWO GENTLEMEN OF VERONA
   (2) Julia